THE NEW YOUNG CHRISTIAN FIELD GUIDE

PRACTICAL ADVICE FOR THE MODERN DISCIPLE

THE NEW YOUNG CHRISTIAN FIELD GUIDE

PRACTICAL ADVICE FOR THE MODERN DISCIPLE

ALAN PASTIAN

TNYC PRESS
— ST. PAUL, MN —

Cover design, illustrations, layout by Erik Swenson Design Co.
(erikswensondesign.com)

Published by TNYC PRESS
A division of The New Young Christian
www.thenewyoungchristian.com

ISBN 978-1-7350734-0-8

Note: In certain instances other translations used and should be noted when possible.

Because of the dynamic nature of the Internet, any web addresses or links contained in this book may have changed since publication.

To my wife Heidi, my daughter Anja and my son Magnus who have made faith the adventure we always believed it could be. We will always be The Pastian Commotion.

Alan Pastian has created an insightful guide for youth and young adults to navigate the complicated terrain of faith and culture. This is a must-read for anyone leading this generation of Christians!

SAM GROSSO, Lead Youth Pastor Victory Church

Alan Pastian's desire to inspire and encourage this generation of young adults as a 'father in the faith' is expressed and felt throughout this book. What he's written is a vital guide for your nexts steps in growing deeper with God.

JOSIAH KENNEALY, Young Adult Director at MNAOG

Alan makes a timely impact with this book as he is passionate to see a generation align their hearts with Christ's. To that end, this book is an informative and practical look at what it means to follow Jesus as a disciple living as a member of the global community in the 21st century. I am confident that, as a result of reading this book, every individual will discover a God-oriented process that will inevitably bring a local impact in their lives.

TERRY PARKMAN, Next Generation Pastor River Valley Church

CONTENTS

0

INTRODUCING

MAKING INTRODUCTION SO IT'S NOT AWKWARD

For those of you that know me and what The New Young Christian is about, welcome to our first book. But for those of you that are meeting me for the first time…let's make some introductions. I was 22 when I found myself surrounded by cardboard moving boxes wondering, "how did I get here?" I had just finished moving into my apartment in the south metro of Minneapolis the night before. I would typically have spent my Saturday nights out with friends, in the pubs, then to the club and finally the after-party. But this weekend I was determined NOT to partake of my typical twenty-something "shenanigans." Because this weekend I was making a change.

I was going to church.

Yeah, that's a strange thing to decide on a Saturday night. I hadn't really stepped into church since I was 13. I found myself drawn back into this particular sacred place that didn't seem to have much relevance for me back then but strangely seemed to be calling me towards it now. Little did I know that going to church that Sunday morning would change everything about me and inspire me to find myself again. Because somewhere along the way… I'd lost myself. I didn't know who I was or where I was going in life.

Let me explain.

I grew up going to church sporadically. I also attended classes to get "confirmed." While my parents and I were hoping for me to become a religious and moral upstanding young man, my "spiritual transformation" ended up becoming more of a "behavioral modification." Being social, extroverted and passionate about my friends and my weekends, I found myself going to church less and less and going out more and more at an early age. High school gave me a lot of memories with some favorites being in football, band, theater, tennis and weekends with my friends. After graduating high school, I spent my first few years at a university that was very well known for its parties and "letting off academic steam." Over the course of those next few years, I focused on building up my social life by joining a fraternity, campus clubs and spending the weekend with my many friends from these different relational networks I was surrounding myself with.

While being social came easy for me, "being me" was harder. I wanted to be everything to everyone. If they needed me to be "the fun dude," I was that. If they needed me to be the "caring guy," I was also that. If they needed me to be the guy "to go first," I would go. If they needed me to break the rules, I would do it (I even took a book of "get out of school passes" from the teachers desk and gave fake passes for my friends and I to get out of school). I wanted to make sure my friends were happy. If my friends weren't happy,

I took it upon myself to believe it was my fault. This led me to be a people-pleasing, manipulating, self-centered young adult who needed attention and wanted to know that I was "important." My college career left me with below average grades in math but getting straight "A's" in partying, addiction, hook-ups and other "activities" that young adults do in their twenties when away from home for the first time.

I can relate to the son who wanted to spend his inheritance on wild living just like the Bible describes (Luke 15:13). God speaks about a son who wanted to live a life by his rules. He leaves the security and provision of his family and chooses to live from one selfish decision to the next. The Bible calls it "wild living." The word "wild" here literally means "wasting." While I'm all about having the time of your life, that's not what I signed up for. I was "wasting my life."

Many of us can relate to experiences in our lives when we wasted time doing things that are frankly stupid. It's like seeing the trailer for a movie that looks so amazing you purchase the early tickets with confirmed seats only to walk out of the film wanting your money back because it was not what you were expecting. You are left disappointed and frustrated that you spent your last ten bucks on a bad attempt at a story. My story felt like that! While I was hoping for a blockbuster life, I got a "Sharknado" with "B actors." It was a waste of time and investment. I wasted my own life while investing in things that didn't give me a meaningful return; it literally felt like a bad movie. I wasn't happy, I didn't know what direction to head in and I couldn't see a future for myself. The only thing I knew is that I needed a change. A big one.

My mom had become a Christian when I was about 16 years old. Her faith was sincere and she experienced Jesus in a genuine way. I however didn't see the need for or want a faith at that time. Through the rest of high school and college, she was kind and patient with me while I chose to dismiss her gentle nudges towards me to "go back to church." It was during those moments that she would ask me to reconsider faith and to take a deep look at the life and inspiration of Jesus Christ. I didn't take her request seriously until I found myself in a serious place of lacking hope and needing to change. So, while my boxes were stacked and still unpacked from moving, I made it a point to find a church and give faith a chance.

I hadn't taken church seriously or been in church for a long time. Walking into a "spiritual environment" like church was very intimidating, considering how unspiritual I had been recently. I found myself intrigued by the kindness of the people, inspired by the message being spoken, unusually moved by the music that was being played and drawn into the prayers that were prayed. I found myself leaning closer to Jesus, overwhelmed and compelled to change my life. I had experienced Christ in the music, the people, the Scriptures and in the prayer that I prayed that day. I surrendered my life to Jesus. And that was the first day of the rest of my life. Christianity became my life.

Becoming a Christian felt a little like getting airdropped into the land of Oz. I was seeing color for the first time. I found myself in a world full of interesting people, wonderful experiences, new territory to discover and a path for me to explore. I was beginning to navigate this new world while pursuing the "guy behind the curtain" who honestly is "great and powerful" and truly does hold the keys to bring me "home." Heaven is home to me. Following Jesus is my life. Building community to be on the journey with me is what I love. I've never been more certain of who I am and what I'm called to do. God created me and knows me best. He made me with my personality, my gifts and my talents. And I want to help others discover who they are and who God is as well.

I would consider myself a "modern disciple." Or in other words, I am a follower of Jesus in a contemporary world. I like discovering new music on Spotify, going to movies that inspire me to be heroic (Tony Stark is my spirit animal), finding new coffee shops in unique parts of town and building relationships with people that wouldn't be caught dead in church. Christianity doesn't always line up with our friends, our work, our interests or our weekends. That becomes a "rub" that we have to deal with in our soul. When what we are seeing, feeling, hearing and doing is different than what the Bible says and what Jesus wants for our lives...that's the tension and the reason for why you are reading this right now. I am figuring out how to keep Jesus at the center of my world in a world that doesn't have or want Jesus at the center of it.

This book is me processing.

Our contemporary culture and modern faith can come to blows at times. The world and your faith in Jesus Christ will feel the heat of friction in its differences.

When they clash, it can leave us with questions. Culture is asking questions that Christianity knows the answer to but is afraid to speak up about because culture will resist it (and religion will ridicule it). Because of that, culture chooses to search for the answer somewhere else.

Answering the questions the world around us isn't asking is confusing and avoiding the answers the world around us is needing is cowardice. Confusion and cowardice swirl around "outsiders of faith" like a cultural tempest as they are tossed around by waves of spiritual diatribe while drowning in a sea of cultural questions . These unbelievers have no choice but to stay alive by grabbing what's in front of them to keep them afloat.

When Christianity ceases to be the answer to the world then Christians become irrelevant to the world. If you are a Christian and you are reading this, you know our faith isn't irrelevant. As a matter of fact, it's essential and critical. Jesus is not insignificant to the world but necessary to the world. But many young outsiders of faith think Christianity is something. Christians who have the answers should be the one's pressing into the communities, colleges, and cities and being the answer the world is looking for.

I currently have built a discipleship platform called The New Young Christian. Think of this as a "home base" for you that focuses on personal inspiration and spiritual formation for today's Christian. We are "New" because our social, cultural, relational and political landscapes are changing. How we choose to engage with our community and culture will determine how we change it.

The message of Jesus Christ is the same but the methods are different.

We are "Young" because we are a new generation of Christians in need of discipleship to discover our design and fulfill our purpose as we declare the good news of a good future for everyone. We are "modern disciples" living in the 21st century desiring to know God and love others with authenticity while discovering our true purpose. It has never been more critical to engage in honest, meaningful and life-giving conversations about faith as we are living out our calling, living in our community and living from our culture.

We are "Christian" because our passion is Jesus, our marching orders are love and our heart is global as we follow Christ into the good and the bad, taking others with us. We are determined to follow Christ beyond a one-time decision of accepting Jesus into a life-long journey of discipleship with Jesus by loving the Bible, building the church and believing Jesus is everything He says He is. We will encounter Christ regularly to be an encounter of Christ to others regularly.

This field guide is your clarity.

These pages are here to reveal to you that you are necessary, that you are part of a greater story.

There is a narrative that you were always meant to be a part of. This story that you are a part of started long before you knew it existed and before you existed:

"Before I formed you in the womb I knew you, before you were born I set you apart; I appointed you" (Jeremiah 1:5)

"Even before He made the world,God loved us and chose us" (Ephesians 1:4)

"You saw me before I was born. Every day of my life was recorded in Your book. Every moment was laid out before a single day had passed" (Psalm 139:1)

This field guide is revealing that you are important. That you are needed. Life's too short and you're too gifted. You're essential but you just don't know it yet. This is your official invitation that you are called to something beyond yourself and that you can't just silently stand by and watch things happen around you. Instead, you are meant to stand up and pray for things to happen through you. This is your opportunity to unearth, excavate, and dig to find answers. When we do, we find we have power. We have virtues. We have strength. We have significance. This leads us to right wrongs and battle against everything that would hold us back from the future we are meant for. What you will discover is that you do have the answers the world needs because of Jesus and these answers are powerful. Almost too powerful. Because once these answers are discovered, they will compel you to go. They will inspire you to seek upward to see and hear from our Creator. They will urge you to go deeper into your communities, to see your relationships become the reliable, trustworthy and life-giving bonds you have always dreamed they could be.

They drive you forward into culture to shape it, transform it and create it.

The New Young Christian is a tribe of young believers on a quest. When we discover what we're living for we know what we're fighting for. Our search for answers leads us to understand "who I am matters." Our quest for "why I'm here" reveals to us "why the journey makes sense." Our inquiries affirm that our journey has significance. Because when God's moving, we move and we are in the center of it. The New Young Christian cares less about where we have been and cares more about where we are going. We will be the first in. We won't stop till we get through it and we will be the most passionate while we do it. You will hear us. You will see us. We will look different and we will sound different because we must love differently than others have seen and heard before.

The New Young Christian is on a journey. We are advancing forward and on mission: to live out our calling, live for our communities and live from our culture. Your calling, your community and your culture are three specific areas you are meant to influence no matter who you are, where you live and what you do. Living out your calling answers the question, "Why am I here?"; living for your community answers the question, "How do I relate? Living from the culture answers the question: "How can I make a difference?" These questions give us forward motion for our faith journey.

LIVING OUT YOUR CALLING

Many are called but few are chosen. We are few because in a noisy world, it's hard to hear. So, we choose to silence the voices that tell us who we are not; tell us why we can't; tell us now is not the time; what we can't do; tell us we don't have it in us. Those voices don't have power over us. We refuse to give them volume. Who we listen to matters. Who we invite in is important. Inspiration, when you break it down, means "spirit in." We say "yes" to the presence of God in us to move us to action. We were made to contain God's Spirit and the Holy Spirit calls out to us, speaks to us and reminds us of who we are and what we are meant to do. When we discover who we were made to be, we will refuse to be anyone else. Being the most authentic and original you is what God is looking for and what the world is waiting for.

LIVING FOR YOUR COMMUNITY

You were never meant to do life alone. Who you surround yourself with is important. Community without natural chemistry is forced, uninteresting and lacks energy. But a community that accepts you compels you to be you. You were always meant to be genuinely and authentically loved. The question you need to ask yourself is this: Is this a safe place for me to be myself? Authenticity dismantles who others want you to be and enhances who you were always meant to be. We are all made unique. You are not mimicked, fabricated or copied but are being restored back to who God always had in mind. From the beginning, no fingerprint is the same. God doesn't mass-produce but He "master-pieces" us together. He crafts each of us uniquely which means when we gather together, no two communities will ever be the same. Each of us carries our own gifts, talents and perspectives so that we can be used by God to speak life, perspective and future over each other and into each other. Each person is a gift, opened up in our communities so that others can enjoy the unique talents and excitement of each unique expression of God's handiwork. Your relationship with others reveals God's creativity and reveals your originality. You will never be fully alive when you are fully alone. God makes community a priority and so do we. The need for relationship is the vehicle for biblical discipleship. Friendship is essential. The Church is critical. The essence of God's Kingdom is our relational connectedness to one another. No one can worship God like you or for you. When you aren't who you were meant to be, we all lack. So, we choose to be who God made us to be, we become who we are supposed to be: the change agents in our neighborhoods, schools, workplaces, churches and cities.

LIVING FROM YOUR CULTURE

We believe culture was meant to be transformed. We don't see secular or sacred. We simply see an opportunity for change. A changed life changes culture. Whether you are a pop artist or a professional worship leader, your gifting redeemed under Jesus gives you an authority to change the culture for Jesus. If you are an actor in movies or making movies on your iPhone in your backyard, we believe films can be transformed into parables, pop songs become worship songs and poets become prophets. We think cultural lines are meant to be crossed. Because Jesus crossed lines. And He did more than cross lines … He removed them. So do we. We don't see us vs them but we see "we." Because "we" is better than "me." We love recklessly because we've been forgiven unreasonably. We will inspire the masses, share convictions and secure the future. We love without agenda or with no strings attached to show the world we won't be held back. Love can't be stopped and neither can we as Christians. So we will go into the most difficult places in culture and watch Jesus transform it into something beautiful.

The New Young Christian doesn't want clichés but passionate, sincere and vulnerable encounters with Christ. We don't want surface relationships with others that produce shallow answers, but we want deep community that promotes the virtues of Christ and cultivates the character to Christ. We don't want to be in a culture war but to be a transformer of culture. When we stop looking to Christ we stop looking to Christianity. So we choose to turn our eyes upon Jesus. Jesus chose to challenge the systems in the current day and create a new way to think and live for all mankind. So do we. Jesus chose to live unapologetically and love unreasonably. So do we.

This field guide is meant to inspire you to love, to live and to lead as a Christian in whatever circle of influence you find yourself in.

Now that you know who I am and what The New Young Christian is about, we want this Field Guide to make you stop and do a double take; to stop you in your tracks and move in a different direction; to get you to make changes in your life for the better, to move forward and to move deeper into faith. Choose today to take the first step. Each single step forward adds up in incremental steps to become advancement...to become your "forward motion" for your own faith journey.

I regularly write posts in our leadership journal on our home base at **thenewyoungchristian.com**. These posts are written as a response to the questions and conflicts that myself and others are having as we are living in and leading forward this new generation of Christians. These posts are modified and collected here in this book. It has never been more critical to engage in honest, meaningful and life-giving conversations about faith and culture. I hope this book gives you language and meaning for your mission to see Jesus lifted up in everything you do.

Thanks for reading and I hope you are inspired!

ALAN

1

FOLLOWING

FOLLOWING JESUS WHEN WE DON'T FEEL LIKE IT

Let's be honest, there are times when it is really easy to follow Jesus, and then there are times when it is really difficult.

For example, when I am in a worship service and the song is moving me and drawing me in to worship on a deeper level…it's easy to follow Jesus.

When I am sitting on my patio with a cup of coffee in my hands reading my Bible with my favorite worship album playing through my airpods…it's easy to follow Jesus.

When my family is healthy, my job is secure and my friendships are life-giving…it's easy to follow Jesus.

But then there are times when it's really hard to follow Jesus.

When someone is driving in the fast lane when they should be in the slow lane…

When someone is standing in front of me with 12 items in the 10 items or less lane …

When someone is talking behind my back and then I have to look at them the next day in the office and forgive them for it…

When I get a Doctor's report that isn't what I was praying for or hoping for...

When my marriage has more tension in it than I ever wanted it to have...

Those moments (and many more) make it hard to follow Jesus. There will be times in life when you are "just not feeling it." When you don't feel like God loves you, cares for you, is with you or wants what's best for you. We love those moments when we feel God's presence and are aware of His love in our lives. But that doesn't happen all the time. And when that doesn't happen, or in other words, when we don't feel like it, what do we do?

We know those moments in life when we aren't feeling it:

When I'm reading Scriptures and they are supposed to be the life-giving Words of God, but they just feel like words on a page to me... When I'm praying to God who is my Creator, but it just seems like I'm talking to myself...

When I'm worshiping in church and others around me are enjoying God, but I just seem to be singing a song and I begin to wonder if this is all real anyway...

When I'm told that God loves me like a Father, but I feel like He's mad at me and no where to be found...

There are times when it's hard to follow God. And if I am being honest, there is a simple reason for my discontent: I don't feel like I love God. I don't feel like worshiping. I don't feel like reading my Bible. I don't feel like going to church. I don't feel like praying. I am simply not feeling it; and I don't think God is feeling it, either. I don't feel He cares about my prayers, my needs or even my life.

And here's the really difficult part...

Feelings come across as so genuine.

Feelings usually are so authentic. They are so vivid. They seem so tangible. They seem to validate who I am and what I am doing, which makes them easy to trust.

And they can also be misleading.

For example, there are days and seasons when you feel like you love your spouse and then there are days when you don't feel it, because life happens. You have to clean the house, you have to go to work, you have to change a diaper, you have to pay the bills, you have to get up early, you haven't seen each other in a few days ... and the grind wears on you.

Ask me if I love my wife like I did on our wedding day when we are in the middle of a fight, the answer would be "not feeling it." But ask me if she is the love of my life on Valentine's Day over a steak dinner with both of us looking amazing and I would say "yes!" before you can finish the question.

Our marital love was a spiritual decision that started on our wedding day. I chose my wife, Heidi, when I knew it and felt it the day I proposed. I chose Heidi on our wedding day when our emotions were high, our tears were real and our vows were heard when we said, "till death do us part." Choosing her during the good times when we feel our love and our romance is usually easiest and most obvious (our anniversary, date nights, walks, etc). But choosing her during the times when I don't feel it confirms and affirms a love that I couldn't see before, making our love more visible and more tangible to me.

Marriage reality here, I don't feel like I love her when I am in the middle of installing the toilet in my basement. I don't feel like I love her when I had a bad day at work, I'm stressed out and I am wanting to simply chill and relax. I don't feel like I love her when we are fighting about how I didn't stack the dishes the right way in the dishwasher. Even though I am not "feeling the love" in those moments, I still acknowledge that our love has meaning, it has purpose and is still important. We have fought about stupid things and important things throughout our life together. But I refuse to let my feelings dictate my marriage; instead I let our choice we made 22 years ago in front of our family and friends on the marriage altar remind me that she's the one, and all I need. I have chosen to commit myself to her even when my feelings don't always match up. The reality is our marriage is a choice I made for life and my love for my wife goes beyond my feelings to the truth that we will be together for life.

Similarly, there are days I don't feel like I love God. The same issues of life and pressures of the day try to steal my emotional connection to God. But I know I am in a love relationship with God that isn't based on how I feel that day, but based upon the faith that God gave me 28 years ago. So, I trust my covenant with Him more than I trust my feelings about Him.

So does all this mean that I shouldn't feel emotion or be emotional?

No.

God is emotional and has feelings.

If we are made in God's image, then we also are

emotional beings and are supposed to have feelings. Here's how God feels about emotional things:

- God feels anger (Psalm 7:11; Romans 1:18)
- God expresses laughter (Psalm 37:13; Psalm 2:4)
- God feels compassion (Psalm 135:14)
- God feels grief (Genesis 6:6; Psalm 78:40; Luke 19:41-44)
- God feels love (1 John 4:8; John 3:16)
- God feels hate (Psalm 5:5; Psalm 11:5)
- God feels joy (Zephaniah 3:17)

God came into our world and as a result knows every temptation, feels every conviction and knows every emotion we will experience; etc. The difference is that He didn't sin while feeling everything we felt (Hebrews 4:15). That's what makes God so trustworthy and understanding about your emotions and your feelings about a situation; He knows what you're going through emotionally because He is emotional. He made you emotional and He knows what emotions you're feeling right now.

You were never meant to live from emotion to emotion. However , you are supposed to live from faith to faith (Romans 1:17), strength to strength (Psalm 84:7), grace to grace (John 1:16), not from feeling to feeling. Living from faith to faith makes you a believer. Living from strength to strength makes you a follower of Jesus. Living from grace to grace is what it's like to be living spiritually as a Christian. If you live from feeling to feeling though, you are in danger of "emotional living." Emotional living is the opposite of a spiritual life in Jesus or "spiritual living."

So how do you know if you are in "emotional living" or living the spiritual life God has for you?

Here are some signs of "Emotional Living"

SIGN 1: I DON'T FEEL GOD, SO GOD IS MAD AT ME OR DOESN'T WANT ME.

Emotional living says if you don't feel God then God is either mad at you or has stopped caring about you; He doesn't want you anymore. Spiritual living understands nothing can separate you from the love of Christ (Romans 8:35).

SIGN 2: I'M FEELING IT, SO I BETTER JUMP IN AND JUST DO IT.

Emotional living leads you in the wrong direction; because what if what you are feeling right now just isn't true? You make a decision out of emotion and now you're possibly heading in the wrong direction. Spiritual living however relies on God's wisdom and counsel, and chooses not to make abrupt, hasty decisions but instead calculated and prayerful ones based on the wisdom of God and with the right counsel.

SIGN 3: I FEEL IT'S RIGHT, SO IT MUST BE TRUE.

Emotional living doesn't tell the truth. Emotional living wants your emotions to speak first and then let truth back up what you're feeling. But spiritual living relies on Scripture to confirm and affirm the truth of a situation despite what you may be feeling.

SIGN 4: I FEEL IT STRONGLY, SO THIS MUST BE MY REALITY.

Emotional living leads you to believe that the only tangible and reliable evidence of your faith is your tears, your joy, etc. Spiritual living understands that what you feel right now is not always what is actual.

SIGN 5: I FEEL LIKE I AM THE ONLY ONE THAT UNDERSTANDS WHAT I AM GOING THROUGH BECAUSE NO ONE ELSE FEELS THE WAY I DO.

Emotional living makes you think your feelings are unique to you and that no one in your community could possibly understand; it isolates you from those who could help you the most. Spiritual living relies on your community for support and prayer to help you navigate the decision or the season.

SIGN 6: I DON'T FEEL LIKE PRAYING OR READING MY BIBLE, SO GOD MUST NOT BE REAL.

Emotional living makes your spiritual life dependent on having a feeling to back up every spiritually good desire. Spiritual living has an understanding that faith is critical for moments when you don't feel like it, and that faith will sustain you until the next time you do.

Having a thriving spiritual life in Jesus isn't void of feelings. Spiritual living relies on feelings to affirm and confirm what God is doing, but refuses to make feelings the primary source of God's will for your life. The primary source of God's will for your life is and always will be obedience.

Jesus made that absolutely clear when He said if we love Him we will obey Him (John 14:15–31). What does this thriving spiritual life of obedience which goes beyond feelings looks like?

Spiritual living looks like this: When you open your Bible or your devotional for the day but it's not what you want to hear and you simply aren't "moved by it" but you read the Scriptures anyhow because you know when you seek first the things of God, somehow it becomes what you needed that day or what your friends needed (Matthew 6:33).

Spiritual living looks like this: When you go to church to worship Jesus and the worship leader asks you raise your hands. You don't feel like raising your hands because the song isn't moving you like everyone else and raising your hands wouldn't be genuine and true to what you are feeling in that moment. But you raise your hands out of obedience to God because your worship isn't dependent on how you feel (or what others are feeling) but it is dependent on who God is and always will be (Psalm 134:2).

Spiritual living looks like this: When you pray for your friend to be healed but the doctor's report says otherwise. Now your prayers feel as if they have no effect but you know that Jesus said to ask, seek and knock for doors to be opened (Matthew 7:7). It may not make sense to you now, but somehow God will have it all make sense in the end (Romans 8:28).

Following Jesus when you don't feel like it will likely be one of the first tests you walk through when you start to follow Christ, and these testing moments will continue.

Matthew 26:33–35 speaks about Peter who became a great example of a Christian whose emotions and obedience were in alignment. Peter was invested and committed to following Jesus and doing ministry with Jesus to the point that he said these words:

> "'Even if everyone runs away because of You, I will never run away!'
>
> 'I assure you,' Jesus said to him, 'tonight, before the rooster crows, you will deny me three times!'
>
> 'Even if I have to die with you,' Peter told Him, 'I will never deny you!' And all the disciples said the same thing.'"

At this point Peter and all the disciples are obediently following Jesus as closely as possible. They are emotionally charged with passion and excitement for who Jesus is and what they will do for Him. We can relate! We can relate to our own moments like this. When we follow Christ with our passions and our own exciting, "I will never deny you" moments; when we're at a worship experience and we are shouting out loud with all we have that "God, you can have my life!"; when we are sharing our faith at a coffee shop boldly and fearlessly; when we pray with someone at school or work and we don't care what others around us think.

While Peter may have been sincere in saying those words, his emotions ultimately did not carry him through to obedience. Because when the test came, Peter ends up denying Jesus. We can all relate to those moments in life when we felt passionate about Jesus, our calling, His belief in us and our future in Christ. But when the decision comes to choose Jesus ... we deny Him. And we feel like a failure. We hear our own "crowing roosters" in the background (Matthew 26:34) when we make promises to God that we will get up early to read our Bibles and pray but we keep hitting snooze again and again. Or when we promise to not go to that website, look at those pictures, get back into that relationship again or go too far sexually with our significant other yet we find ourselves looking, participating and crossing the line yet again. While this can seem and feel disappointing to Peter (and us), there is a resolution that comes.

In John 2, Peter, like us, is in the middle of a moment where his own feelings about himself and how Jesus felt about him were misguided, not truly reflecting who Peter is and who Jesus is. But Jesus will not allow Peter (or you) to stay spiritually incongruent for long:

"After breakfast Jesus asked Simon Peter, 'Simon son of John, do you love me more than these?' 'Yes, Lord,' Peter replied, 'you know I love you.' 'Then feed my lambs,' Jesus told him. Jesus repeated the question: 'Simon son of John, do you love me?' 'Yes, Lord,' Peter said, 'you know I love you.' 'Then take care of my sheep,' Jesus said. A third time he asked him, 'Simon son of John, do you love me?' Peter was hurt that Jesus asked the question a third time. He said, 'Lord, you know everything. You know that I love you.' Jesus said, 'Then feed my sheep'" (John 21:15–17).

Peter most likely felt Jesus didn't love him ... but He did. Peter probably felt Jesus was mad at him ... but He wasn't. Peter might have felt he wasn't worthy ... but he was. Peter felt he was unforgiven ... but he wasn't. Peter felt he wasn't worthy to be a disciple (he even went back to his old life of fishing) ... but he was. Peter didn't feel like "the rock," but he realized in that moment that how we feel about ourselves and how we feel about God isn't always true. Peter's misguided feelings were finally aligned with God! Peter obeys God from that moment forward to follow the command of Christ when He said, "Feed my sheep."

Soon after this conversation and revelation, we get to one of the best highlights from Peter's ministry. He is preaching and literally thousands come to Christ (Acts 2). He is passionately feeling it and purposefully obeying the call of God on his life that Jesus had spoken over him in his very early days, "Upon this rock (Peter) I will build my church" (Matthew 16:18).

It's clear from our story of Jesus and Peter that obedience and feelings don't always line up. When we don't feel it but we are doing it, it's like our feelings are dragging. Maybe I'll say it this way...

Our feelings have to catch up to our obedience.

Peter was with Jesus. He was following Him from the boat to the shore, talking and eating with Him again ... just like the old days. Was he feeling the love? No. But was he doing what Jesus asked? Yes. Jesus made the call to Peter to have friendship with Him and eat together again. Peter obediently follows Christ to the shore and we begin to see Christ take away Peter's feelings of rejection and replace them with the truth of Jesus' restoration.

"Jesus said to them, 'Bring some of the fish you have caught.' So Simon Peter climbed back into the boat and dragged the net to shore. It was full of large fish. Jesus said to them, 'Come and have breakfast.' None of the disciples dared ask him, 'Who are you?' They knew it was the Lord. Jesus came, took the bread and gave it to them, and did the same with the fish" (John 21:10-13).

Sometimes Jesus will call us closer to Him for friendship, to pray, to love, to worship, to give, to follow, and we just need to obey because eventually our feelings will catch up to His call. Not only will we be doing the work of Jesus, but we will be feeling it as well. Jesus said it best:

"My sheep listen to my voice; I know them, and they follow me. I give them eternal life, and they will never perish; no one can snatch them away from me" (John 10:27–28).

Just as Peter denied Jesus three times when the rooster crowed, Jesus asked Peter three times if he loved Him. Peter's response is what he should have known from the beginning and what we should know in our own moments of denial and failure:

"Lord, you know..." (John 21:17).

Jesus knows us inside and out. He knows that there are times we are going to follow whole-heartedly and not think twice about His love for us and our love for Him. Then there are times when we will sincerely want to follow and do the right thing, but we don't. It's in these moments when our feelings compel us to hold up, give up and not show up. And it's in these moments that we can't allow our feelings to get the better of us. Because our feelings are very good at sabotaging our faith. Before they do, hear the call to go back to the shore of restoration so you can have that friendship with Jesus again.

So how do we not let our feelings get the better of us?

1: REMIND YOURSELF THAT A LOSS OF FEELING DOESN'T MEAN A LOSS OF FAITH.

I don't call my dad every day. If I don't feel like I love my father every day it doesn't mean he doesn't love me every day. I see my dad a few times a year, but our love doesn't change. God is my perfect Father and I'm His son. Nothing can change that. God is not a Father who abandons and leaves you orphaned. Quite the contrary. He adopts you into His family and nothing can separate you from His love (Romans 8:15, 31–39). So if you feel like God doesn't love you, trust in the strong bond of the Father's love that He will not leave you; even you cannot make the decision to remove yourself from Him! He's your Father and He loves you unconditionally.

2: BE ALL IN WITH GOD BECAUSE GOD IS ALL IN WITH YOU.

You may not always believe in you, but God always believes in you. What He starts He finishes. The good work He begins in you is also the faithful work He completes in you (Philippians 1:6). He's not like me when I'm trying to put together one of those 10,000-piece puzzles. After I build it for a while—I might complete the border—then I'm out. I'm not the guy who has the puzzle on the table for six weeks, delightfully shuffling over to the 10,000 piece nightmare and says to himself 'This is so relaxing' as he stares into a pile of chaos. If I can't finish that puzzle in a day or two, I'm done. But God's not. He never is because He's all in and will finish what He started in you.

3: KNOW THAT HOW GOD FEELS ABOUT ME IS DIFFERENT THAN HOW I FEEL ABOUT MYSELF.

Just because you don't feel like you are worthy doesn't mean God doesn't think you are. Just because you don't think you're worth the fight doesn't mean God isn't fighting for you right now. Your perceptions and feelings about yourself are going to be different than how God feels about you. Trust in who He says you are, not in just what your feelings say you are.

4: RESPOND TO GOD'S PROMISES RATHER THAN REACT TO YOUR FEELINGS.

God makes these promises to you; read them and believe them when you don't feel like worshiping, praying or seeking God:

"When you seek Him with all your hearts you will find Him" (Jeremiah 29:13).

"When you press on to know Him, He will come to you like spring rain" (Hosea 6:3).

"When you come to Jesus, your heart hunger will be satisfied" (John 6:35).

5: REMIND YOURSELF THAT WHEN WE ARE FAITHLESS GOD IS FAITHFUL.

Even though I may not be loving God like I should every day, God is still loving me. 2 Timothy 2:13 says, "If we are faithless he remains faithful, for he cannot disown himself." In the midst of our uncertainty He is certain to be with us no matter what.

6: DO WHAT YOU USED TO DO.

When was the last time you were "on fire for God?" What were you doing during those times that gave you passion to keep going? Were you reading your Bible, spending time in prayer, hanging with other Christian friends, sharing your faith? Reverse engineer those moments of powerful intimacy for you and do what you did then. Because when you start doing those things again, your feelings change and your spiritual life will come alive.

7: WALK BY FAITH AND NOT BY SIGHT.

We walk by sight. We walk by hearing. We walk by feelings. But God's best for us is to walk by faith as often as we can (2 Corinthians 5:7). Obedience is a visible expression of our faith. So follow God in obedience and see Him more than you ever thought you could.

8: DON'T LIVE PASSIVELY.

The key here is refusing to be passive and making a conscious decision to do what's right. Being passive means you wait for an outside force to move you or to make you feel like doing something. Use your will to choose what's right, and pray for God's grace to give you the ability to do it.

Obedience and feelings will be at odds with each other at times. But our feelings can't be the driving force behind our decisions, our actions and our beliefs. Building your decisions based on how you feel will result in a fragile and confusing life that can be redirected because of the weather or how good or bad a weekend you had recently. Be mature to know when your feelings aren't in alignment to your faith and experience the true life of following Jesus into a future that is more meaningful than you could have asked or thought!

CHAPTER 1 QUESTIONS

1. Is it easier to live by feelings or by faith? Why?

2. How does it make you feel when you discovered that God is emotional?

3. Which sign of "emotional living" relates most to you?

4. How can you relate to Peter's denial of faith in your own life?

5. Do you believe the words, "your feelings have to catch up to your obedience"? Why or why not?

2

OVERCOMING

OVERCOMING INSECURITY AND GETTING YOUR CONFIDENCE BACK

We have all experienced moments in our lives when we have lost our confidence. That moment when we felt like we weren't going to succeed. That moment when we thought "someone else should be doing this, not me." Every person has or will experience moments in their lives where they don't trust themselves and they lose confidence. I have discovered that this loss of confidence, this insecurity, will come when you compare yourself to another person. Because when you compare yourself, you ultimately doubt yourself.

I doubt my myself in the gym. I have friends who are trainers, successful college athletes and even models who make the gym a way of life. I only go there if I have to. So I attempt to make up for my athletic shortcomings with my workout gear. At least I can try to look the part. So I give my confidence a little boost by wearing the accepted athletic brands in my suburban gym. And in the course of finding the perfect clothing gear for the gym, I've come to realize there are two kinds of people: those that wear workout gear as "everyday clothes" and those that wear their workout gear for the purpose of actual fitness. The first group of people are those who wear fitness gear as part of their everyday life: comfort, laziness, style, brand allegiance, etc. These are confident people! Wearing a compression shirt to Target to pick up toilet paper isn't my thing or what I do. Some will wear their yoga pants all day. They live in them. I don't own yoga pants. But I do own long underwear. I'm convinced it's the "yoga pants" for the dude (I'm from MN and it's a thing here). But wearing your long underwear in public is not cool. So keep it behind closed doors, fellas.

The second group of people are those that wear their gear for one purpose: to work out. That's me. And that gear makes me feel confident. So confident that I walk in and grab my spot on the bench ready to show the "bro's" in the gym I mean business. Only to be interrupted by a dude with no neck who told me that he was already working out here before I got there. I oblige and slide over only to bump into the dude who was grunting pretty loud earlier. I'm an "anti-grunter" because it's awkward. It's not like the grunts intimidate me, but it's the fact that these guys around me look like Thor. I look like Avenger's Endgame Thor (I have a love-hate relationship with carbs). And as I'm there, I begin to think that I don't belong there. That I'm not good enough to be there. Slowly I find myself migrating to the "mat and the balls" doing a few sit-ups and push-ups. My confidence in my bench press has diminished to a pink sit-up ball and a few dumbbells.

What happened to me? Where did my confidence go?

Insecurity seems to develop when a person compares his or herself to another; so don't try to be someone you're not. Be yourself. Realize that who God designed you to be is not a mistake. You need to stop comparing and start living in your own skin. And if you wear workout gear as everyday clothes, then wear those compression shirts with confidence!

Let me give you some insights on overcoming insecurity and growing in confidence.

1: THERE IS A CORRELATION BETWEEN MY RELATIONSHIP WITH JESUS AND MY INSECURITY WITH OTHERS

If you have uncertainty in your relationship with God then you will have uncertainty in your relationships with others. But the opposite is also true: the more secure you are in the presence of God, the more secure you are in the presence of YOU and others. You will never be more confident than when you are in the presence of God. It's in God's presence you are reminded that you are loved, you are necessary and you have a future.

Insecurity is normal. It plagues all of us. Those moments when we wonder if what we are doing is worth it, did we miss it and are we doing what we were meant to do? I remember when I started my own design company. I always felt like I was supposed to be an entrepreneur. I wanted to try my hand at owning a business. It was small and I had a staff of a few people. My team and I started designing for churches and other companies. God brought projects our way and we were creating. God showed me that I was a creator, just like Him. But as business picked up, so did the criticism. Even though I think it looked awesome, not everyone else did. The voices got into my head that I wasn't creative anymore. That my design eye was "flawed" and I questioned what I was doing and who I was! But there was a unique correlation between this moment in my life and my spiritual life. As business picked up my quiet time went down. I had to make calls in the morning, many times early, due to time differences and because of my other job as a pastor. So I started missing my times with God. And when I missed those times with God, I missed God reminding me that I am loved by Him. When I became too busy to connect with God, I lost my source of creativity which always is God. When I put my design work ahead of my prayer time, I lost my identity as a leader and that what I was doing was making a difference. This is why I'm now so passionate about spending time in worship, reading the Bible and prayer. It's in these moments I am reminded of who I am and what I am supposed to do with my life. The world will always have an opinion about you, your appearance, your work, your style, your speaking, etc. When I am in the presence of God, He always points me back to who I am and what I am meant to do. Never forget when it seems as though the odds are always against you, remember that God is always for you. The presence of God is the most secure place you can be as a Christian.

2: BEING INSECURE IS WHEN I FOCUS ON WHAT OTHERS THINK ABOUT ME INSTEAD OF WHAT GOD THINKS ABOUT ME.

Here's the difference between being an insecure person and a secure person; insecurity is when I'm focused on what others think about me, but security is when I'm focused on what God thinks about me. When you truly find out how God made you to be, and your identity in Him, you will never want to be anyone else or do anything else. Confidence is being sheltered in the will of God. God's will is both "who you are" and "what you do." God's will is about you becoming the right person first, then doing the right tasks second. Who you are in Him will always precede what you do.

When you stop comparing yourself to others and cease striving to have someone else's calling, but instead determine to be yourself according to how God made you, your confidence will conquer. I've realized this: the moment I start depending on what others think of me is the moment I start doubting what God can do with me. The most confident moments you'll experience in your life are moments when you are most secure in Christ's definition of who you are and what He's called you to do.

Remember, "You can do all things through Christ who gives you strength" (Philippians 4:13). You can do all He calls you to do, because He will equip you for His call – and strengthen you when you need strength the most. If you are facing insecurity in your leadership and life, remember today "He who calls you is faithful, He will surely do it" (1 Thessalonians 5:24).

3: CONCENTRATE ON MY ABILITIES.

What are you good at doing? Make a list of your good qualities. You probably have more than you think you do. In times of feeling insecure we often forget who we are and how God has shaped us through experiences of life. Imagine telling a family member or a friend they aren't gifted. So why would we believe this about ourselves? Make a list and keep it accessible. It will help you feel more confident if you focus more on your positives than your negatives.

4: NEVER STOP GROWING.

Seek wisdom from other leaders who have gone before you. I love that the Bible is full of leaders who felt unqualified and who were lacking the skills and education to do the job. When I feel overwhelmed or insecure, I read the stories like those of Gideon, Moses, Joseph, David or Joshua to supply me with great encouragement for the journey. Find knowledge from mentors who are further down the road than you. Read books on topics that interest you and from authors you want to mimic or learn from. Up your education. Join a network. The more you grow in information the more competent you will feel in your role.

5: INSECURITY ALWAYS REARRANGES WHAT I SEE AND HEAR IN LIFE.

Discover God's perspective first. Insecurity will distort what you see and hear. So maybe the chaos you're experiencing in your family, friendships, at work, etc. is because you are focusing your eyes on the wrong things or listening to the wrong voices. If God holds everything together then being held by God means you should be the most secure person in the room; and if security is being held by God, then insecurity could mean that you were feeling out of the grip and hand of God in those moments. While nothing can separate us from the love of God as a Christian, you can still feel like you are not loved by God. Never stop going back to the presence of God; if you do not quit, you'll never experience deep insecurity again.

The root of confidence is always going to be where you put your trust. Pride says, "I've got this." Confidence says, "God's got this." Biblical confidence is rooted in obedience to what God is calling you to do. Pride is rooted in arrogance about what you are wanting to do. The Bible asks a question, "Why so down and lacking confidence, put your trust in God" (Psalm 42:5). Whom you put your trust in, where you focus, the voices you listen to, determine how you progress forward.

6: WHETHER I REALIZE IT OR NOT, GOD TRUSTS ME MORE THAN I TRUST MYSELF.

You are called to do great things. That's not a leadership cliché' but a truth from Jesus who reminds us "Greater things you will do because I go to the Father" (John 14:12). I think that's why I love James and John arguing over who is greatest in the kingdom (Luke 9:46). Basically "who is more awesome, me or you?" was the argument Christ had to settle.

Notice Jesus didn't shut them down for their confidence but simply asked them if they had what it takes to do the big things God called them to do. Spending time with Christ on a regular basis allows Him to bring the greatness in you to the surface for you to discover, and it also brings the confidence to do what God is calling you to do.

7: TRUST THE RIGHT SOURCE.

Let's define confidence for a moment by defining what it is not. Confidence is not arrogance. There is a difference. Arrogance is an overbearing pride and extreme self-importance. Confidence is a trustworthy reliance and belief in someone or something.

The word confidence has a word embedded in it that is critical to being confident and overcoming insecurity. It's the word "confide." True biblical confidence is found when we confess our brokenness and trust in Christ. It's easy for people, especially driven people, to put their trust in their network, their title, their pay-check, their personality. But the second we lose any of those, we lose our confidence as well.

When we intentionally put ourselves in the place of regular repentance, when we are vulnerable with our fears and insecurities, when we place our trust back into God's hands and take it out of our hands, that's when our confidence is strengthened. Practically speaking, the more you are in God's presence, reading God's word and speaking regularly to God, letting God fill you, letting God inspire you, the more confident you will be.

Confidence is not what you do with God but what God does with you. Confidence is what keeps you grounded securely in God. Don't limit God by your insecurity. It's in the presence of God that you will find the affirmation for the task. When God affirms you, it's to remind you and place you in extreme security in Him.

8: FIND PEOPLE WHO COMPLIMENT MY WEAKNESSES.

A healthy church or organizational strength comes from its different people. So don't be afraid to ask for help. There are people who are better at doing things you don't feel comfortable doing or are not skilled at doing. It's not a sign of weakness to get others involved. It's actually a sign of strength as a leader.

Followers of Jesus who are insecure and lacking confidence are sensitive about their positions. They are defensive of their performance in work situations, leadership situations, etc. They are constantly aware of other's authority and try to control others around them to protect their position, performance and authority.

Christians who want to grow in their confidence move from a posture of defensiveness to an offensive position. Confident Christians celebrate other's performance and champion them forward. Confident Christians hold an offensive posture by giving authority and responsibility away to others, allowing the community to celebrate their collective potential.

9: UNDERSTAND THAT I AM A MASTERPIECE.

The world has a message. This message that is speaking to you is at war with how God sees you and how God wants to use you. This "unsacred utterance" is heard in advertising, in TV, in music, etc. It says this: "you are not good enough!" Culture is constantly reminding you of this. It's nagging pull is reminding you constantly that you don't measure up, that you don't fit in, that you are lacking and are incomplete.

We live in a more visual world. We spend more time in front of screens and "looking at ourselves" than ever before. The constant presence of social media in our lives has caused us to be believe the lie that we aren't made good enough. One piece of evidence in proving this cultural lie of "not being good enough" is the rise of cosmetic surgery. According to the American Society of Plastic Surgeons (ASPS), almost 18 million people underwent some form of cosmetic surgery in 2018 and has been rising over the last 5 years. From "mommy makeovers" to a new trend on the rise, "daddy do-overs", culture is speaking a message that we aren't good enough. This adds to the greater false narrative that you aren't smart enough, strong enough, compassionate enough, etc. But God reminds us that we are perfect just the way we are "For we are God's handiwork, created in Christ Jesus to do good works, which God prepared in advance for us to do" (Ephesians 2:10).

This word, "workmanship", is where we get the Greek word "poema." This is obviously where we get our English word, "poem." That means that you are a creative work of God as an artist. You are God's masterpiece...a work of art. God's creation. God is an artist that is forming and painting and writing a masterpiece and He thinks you're amazing just the way you are.

When we had our first child, Anja, she was the most beautiful baby in the world. How did I know this? Because as a pastor, going to the hospital and loving on families and their new bundles of joy that have come into the world is part of the job! And when they would show me their new baby, I would often hear them say, "isn't she the most beautiful baby you have ever seen?" While my smile and nod of my head would say one thing, inside my mind was looking at that baby and I was saying to myself, "Actually, not really. If they would have seen MY daughter, Anja, they would realize that their baby is lacking in a small way in the "cute department." Especially those babies that look like tiny old people. But to the parents, they are the cutest baby in the world! Because it was "made" by that father and that mother.

That's how God feels about you.

You are His child and you are His creation. When you feel insecure, it's because you feel like you aren't enough in the room, in the moment, for the job, for the task, etc. But God thinks otherwise. He made you, with your personality, your gifts and talents to be used by God to make a difference. Be OK with who you are. The world thinks it can define you. But the world didn't create you. God did.

He alone gets to define you. He gets to tell you your worth and your value. Because you are a true work of art.

But many times we simply don't see ourselves as valuable. We don't think we have anything to offer. We don't have any worth. But you were created by God. You are not meant to be thrown away but to be treasured. You are not garbage but a work of art waiting to be discovered.

A New Jersey couple understood this first-hand when they found a painting in the basement of their parent's home. After the homeowners died, their adult children hired Nye and Co. to comb the property for valuables. Combing through the house was a task as their parents had collected a lot of worthless items through the years. But one item they discovered captured their eyes. What they found was not worthless but it was a long-lost painting by Rembrandt. Conservationists discovered Rembrandt's initials on the painting, under a layer of varnish, proving that the painting was indeed his work. John Nye, owner of Nye and Co. auction house in Bloomfield, New Jersey, said "The picture was remarkably unremarkable." A small, slightly damaged oil painting ended up being worth millions. What seemed worthless and was ready to be thrown away actually sold for a reported 3 - 4 million dollars. Sometimes we feel like the discarded painting that gets overlooked and doesn't seem to be worth much. But that couldn't be farther from the truth! You are God's masterpiece- far more valuable than this Rembrandt will ever be!

10: DON'T THROW AWAY MY CONFIDENCE.

We feel worthless when we throw away confidence. God made it clear to not throw away our confidence:

"So do not throw away this confident trust in the Lord. Remember the great reward it brings you!" (Hebrews 10:35).

Confidence is one of the most valuable attributes you can possess. Confidence helps you find that you are necessary and you are more valuable than you think. One more art illustration for you. Da Vinci is a famous artist. I saw his work in Paris when I visited The Louvre. It was here that I saw first hand his famous painting of The Mona Lisa. This is the most expensive painting in the world. The original painting size is 30" x 20 7/8" and is owned by the Government of France. While this piece is truly considered a masterpiece by the world's standard, it didn't come easy. Da Vinci took a total of 7 years to paint the Mona Lisa.

You an imagine some of the 16th century neighbors and friends of Da Vinci. Most lived in the country farming and if they lived in the city they would have been engaged in a wide variety of different trades, blacksmith, carpenter, goldsmith, shoemaker, candle-maker, baker, etc. Da Vinci's friends and family were probably wondering what he had been up to for seven years. Da Vinci's response:

"Creating my masterpiece."

Devoting seven years to a space that was only 30" x 20 7/8", would be considered a "waste of time" to the average person. But to an artist like Da Vinci, he considered it his joy and obsession to create something that the rest of the world now sees as "priceless." He didn't throw away his confidence, but kept pursuing his passion. What was seen by others as a waste of time and space, was actually a valuable use of time and resource.

God is creating masterpieces that the world is saying is not good enough. If the world is trying to tell you that you aren't valuable and you aren't worth the time and effort... God disagrees. God sees you as "one of a kind.' And God's determination of your worth gives you the security to walk into any room and every situation with confidence.

CHAPTER 2 QUESTIONS

1. "Insecurity seems to develop when a person compares his or herself to another." Do you agree with this statement? Why or why not?

2. Is there a correlation with your insecurity in your relationship with Jesus and your security with others?

3. Confidence is not arrogance. There is a difference. Arrogance is an overbearing pride and extreme self-importance. Confidence is a trustworthy reliance and belief in someone or something. How have you battled with the difference between confidence and arrogance?

4. How has culture told you that you don't measure up?

5. Is it hard to see yourself as a masterpiece? Why/why not?

3

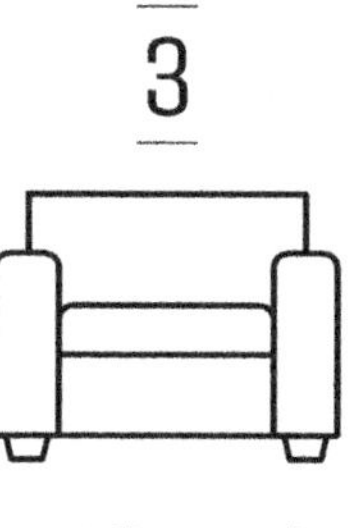

RESTING

RESISTING BALANCE BY BRINGING SABBATH BACK INTO YOUR LIFE

The idea of resting could be a lost art because we've never been more busy than right now. More and more of us are working out of our homes and in coffee shops because of virtual offices. Social media moves us to buy now, go there, eat that, like this and follow them. FOMO (Fear Of Missing Out) is driving us deeper into anxiety to not miss out and fill our schedules to the breaking point. Being encouraged to rest at the right times might be the best leadership advice you could ever receive.

The Bible's word for rest is one we don't hear very often. The word is "Sabbath." When we hear that spiritual word Sabbath we can wonder what it means. It's like the word "Jedi" from Star Wars or "Patronus" from Harry Potter. We hear about it and see it practiced by a few people but we don't really know what it really is or how to experience it.

Sabbath is observed for the first time in the Bible in Genesis 2. "By the seventh day God had finished the work he had been doing; so on the seventh day he rested from all his work" (Genesis 2:2).

Not only does our Creator model to us the power of rest after a busy work week, but God commands it:

> Remember the Sabbath day by keeping it holy. Six days you shall labor and do all your work, but the seventh day is a sabbath to the Lord your God. On it you shall not do any work (Exodus 20:8-10).

God knows how we function. God is our Father and we are His children, so He knows when we need rest to keep going and to avoid having our own "spiritual meltdowns."

As a dad of two teenagers, I can still remember when my kiddos were toddlers. When we were at the park, there came that time when I had to remind them that it was time for them to go home and "take a nap." The idea of rest was not on my daughter's two-year-old radar as we were in the middle of playing "Beauty and the Beast" on the playground. I can recall chasing her down, bringing her home, and putting her in her bed crying and saying these words, "Dad! I'm not tired!" But as a Dad that knows his kids limits, I knew that if I allowed those big beautiful tears to persuade me to keep her awake and skip the nap, we would have a "Target meltdown" on lock for later that day. So I would let her cry out her last bit of playful energy and eventually those wimpers would go silent. In a few hours she was back up again ready for more Disney princess time!

There are times when we are doing life, working hard and in the grind and God gently interrupts our moments with a nudge, "Time to rest." We often respond like my own little kiddos with our chest puffed out and confidently standing there in defiance telling God,

"I'm not tired."

But like a Good Father, He knows what you need. You need the rest. It's for your own good. That's why God put it as a command.

Sabbath comes from the original Hebrew word "sabat," which means literally "to cease and desist." This is a legal and authoritative term that denotes a legally enforceable order from a court or government agency directing someone to stop engaging in a particular activity. Rest from God is not just a suggestion but it's a command. A good command for our own good.

Mark 2:27 says, "The Sabbath was made for man, not man for the Sabbath."

If taking a Sabbath is a command and keeping it holy is in the Ten Commandments, then not resting is a sin. That almost seems weird to read, but it's essentially true. That means to take a nap might be one of the most spiritual things you can do right now.

I'm a doer. I am a dreamer. I want to succeed at my career. I want to help as many people as I can. I want to be the best father. I want to be an amazing husband. I want to check off more on my bucket list. I have many decisions I have to make on a daily basis with my job. My kids need me to help with algebra which I haven't done in two decades. I have hundreds of channels to choose from on my TV, I have thousands of songs to listen to on my iPhone and I have a lot of things coming up on my calendar. So many choices, so many decisions and so much to do.

But God has calls you a "Royal Priesthood" and more specifically, a "chosen generation" (1 Peter 2:9). And a "chosen generation" must master the art of "choosing God" in the midst of a culture where the choice to do so much is constantly bombarding us.

So, where does rest fit into all this?

Rest can come in many forms: reading, naps, binging your favorite shows, poolside vibes, on the couch watching football, eating your favorite meal, spending quality time with friends, etc. The best kind of rest is one that rejuvenates the body, soul and spirit. It rekindles a fire in you again. A Sabbath rest is unique because it's God-initiated and God-inspired and it replenishes us holistically. I don't think this kind of rest has to be as complicated as we make it or so difficult to find.

So here are some practical ways to incorporate a Sabbath mind-set into your daily life:

1: TAKE A 30–60 MINUTE DAILY SABBATH.

Take a 30–60 minute Sabbath in the morning to be committed to reading God's Word and having a time of prayer. It fuels you for the day and it gives you an opportunity to invite God into your meetings and plans before they even start. I always choose to "eat Scripture" before I eat my breakfast—a simple discipline that keeps me on track and committed. "But seek first his kingdom and his righteousness, and all these things will be given to you as well" (Matthew 6:33).

2: TAKE A HALF-DAY SABBATH EACH WEEK.

Take a half-day Sabbath each week, a time to shut off your phone and email; I would suggest about 2–3 hours in your working week. This doesn't mean stop working. For many of us, we are working throughout the week. But it does mean to silence the interruptions and focus without the stressful interruptions. When I worked in Washington, D.C. I would take Wednesday mornings from 9–12, and I would simply lay out my next few weeks and months before God. I would look at my schedule and pray through it. I would keep my journal page open and jot down ideas God would put in mind—Scriptures, faces of those whom I felt I needed to reach out to etc. I would take that time to dream and pray into the plans and projects I was working on. God led the agenda and I simply prayed, listened and wrote down what I thought God was speaking. Great blueprints for my ministry came from these days, and continue to. It's one of the most effective disciplines of my career. No matter what stage of life or career you are in, taking an hour or two to pray into your responsibilities removes the stress and puts your confidence and trust back towards God who called you to the job and the current season you are in.

> Search me, O God, and know my heart; test me and know my anxious thoughts. See if there is any offensive way in me, and lead me in the way everlasting (Psalm 139:23-24).

3: TAKE YOUR WEEKLY SABBATH DAY.

Take your Sabbath day and keep it holy by giving a day to God. On this day, give godly relationships priority, spend quality time with loved ones, seek God together as a family, laugh, eat a great meal, watch a movie, be outside … simply do things that recharge you and energize you. Because relationships invigorate me specifically, I always build into my Sabbath days conversations with those who inspire me, encourage me and build me up. If you're the opposite, build into your day downtime for just you to recharge.

"Observe my Sabbaths and have reverence for my sanctuary. I am the Lord" (Leviticus 26:2).

4: TAKE A MONTHLY SABBATH DAY.

Once a month, set aside time to lay out the names, plans and ideas that you have for your family, career and future to God. If you don't have the flexibility in your schedule to do this during the week, use one of your Sunday's to do this if possible. Use this time intentionally to evaluate, think critically, and make plans. Pray over your family and think seriously about your family's trajectory: financial goals, marriage tune-ups, quality time, etc. Use this time to lay difficult relationships before God and ask if there are any planks in your own eye. Pray into your career path and let God speak to you about ideas, innovations, key relationships and pray for open doors. Pray into future plans so you can see and hear what God's heart is for your future. Take time to pray for others and ask God who needs you to encourage them or pray for them. It's here that I get retreat ideas on paper, family values are inspired, mentorship relationships established, etc. It's not supposed to be work but it is supposed to be establishing vision for my future.

"There remains, then, a Sabbath-rest for the people of God; for anyone who enters God's rest also rests from their works, just as God did from his" (Hebrews 4:9-10).

5: TAKE A YEARLY SABBATH RETREAT.

This doesn't have to be a big production. For me, this is "staycation" style. I do this every year in January. I take a few days to fast, prayer walk in the local parks, hit some of my favorite places that refresh me, spend time with inspiring people and simply let God speak to me. If you're feeling more ambitious, then simply go camping, get a cabin or book a hotel room so you can spend a few days away and grab ahold of God's plans and purposes for your life.

> Come to me, all you who are weary and burdened, and I will give you rest. Take my yoke upon you and learn from me, for I am gentle and humble in heart, and you will find rest for your souls. For my yoke is easy and my burden is light (Matthew 11:28).

What is the result of practicing Sabbath in this way in my life? It's this: I've never experienced burnout. God has put a fire in me from the first day I experienced salvation, and that fire God put in my heart is my responsibility to keep lit. Leviticus 6:12–13 says:

> The fire on the altar must be kept burning; it must not go out. Every morning the priest is to add firewood… the fire must be kept burning on the altar continuously; it must not go out.

I love this Old Testament picture for our modern day faith! Sabbaths are like fuel for the fire in your heart. This is the ultimate expression of "burnout" as a leader and as a Christian: It means you are not keeping your fire going. What keeps you going is what fuels you. Your passions, desires, interests, values, etc are all indicators of what keeps you fueled up and fired up! So when you take a Sabbath incorporate that list above as part of your rest. Watch a movie if good stories stoke your fire. Go out to a great restaurant with friends if food and fellowship inspire you. Spend time alone with your favorite worship songs and walk outside. Go to Barnes and Noble, find your favorite author or devotional and drink coffee and read. It will look different for everyone but find what fuels you up and do it often to keep your fire burning- and to avoid burn out.

These Sabbaths won't just magically happen. You have to get out your calendar and start right now by adding dates and jealously guarding that time. Your calendar shouldn't rule you…you should rule your calendar. Schedule these dates into your calendar and fight to keep them a priority. If it's necessary and appropriate, let your family, superiors, etc. know as well and watch your spiritual life get reignited.

Dallas Willard once called hurry, "the great enemy of spiritual life in our day," and said followers of Jesus must "ruthlessly eliminate hurry." Busy and hurry are always competing for our affection, each promising us fulfillment but never quite delivering and ultimately giving us restlessness which causes us to work even harder and more often. John Mark Comer wrote about this in *The Ruthless Elimination of Hurry:*

> Ultimately, nothing in this life, apart from God, can satisfy our desires. Tragically, we continue to chase after our desires ad infinitum. The result? A chronic state of restlessness or, worse, angst, anger, anxiety, disillusionment, depression—all of which lead to a life of hurry, a life of busyness, overload, shopping, materialism, careerism, a life of more...which in turn makes us even more restless. And the cycle spirals out of control.

As well as practicing the disciplines above, we should also be operating from a place of Sabbath rest daily. Yet how often we operate from a place of striving, frustration, and stress, missing out on the peace God has promised to His followers.

So, how can we learn to operate from a daily position of rest?

---

1. LEARN CONTENTMENT IN EVERYTHING

There is always a draw towards bigger and better. The challenge is to be content with who God made you to be and where God has placed you (Philippians 4:12-13). Comparison kills contentment. Plain and simple. A lack of contentment compels you to do more. So stop comparing yourself, your calling and your successes to everyone else. Your one "yes" to God ultimately means that everyone else and everything else was a "no." God chose you to do what only you can do. That makes your life trajectory different than the others down the street, different than the church down the coast, different than the leader across the ocean. Your obedience will look different than everyone else's around you but the blessing is always guaranteed. If you're going to compare yourself to another person...then compare yourself to Jesus. Obedience is the "spiritual force" that makes you into His likeness and forges a path to your purpose. As you practice contentment by killing comparison you will find yourself operating from a place of rest.

2: MOVE PAST YOUR DISAPPOINTMENT.

You have probably figured out that once you accept Christ, your life doesn't magically get easier. In fact, you're not alone in seeing that life seems to get more difficult and messy. You will have setbacks in life as a Christian. People will disappoint you. As a Christian and as a leader, you will have critics that will show up in your life. It will be easy at times to isolate yourself, wall yourself up, shut down or give up on your faith. Not only that, you won't always understand "why God is allowing this" throughout your life. That disappointment can drain you, frustrate you and even cause you to work harder to "fix" what God didn't do.

I can guarantee this: you won't always fully understand the big picture...but rest assured there is one. There is a greater vision at work that you can't see; that's why you have to write that vision down, simplify it and run hard and fast with it (Habakkuk 2:2). Keep the vision of your calling from God in mind and push forward, regardless of the obstacles which come your way. Rather than "losing your peace" over disappointments, move past your disappointment and you will find rest.

3: SEEK WISDOM FIRST.

If you haven't read Proverbs in a while, read it. The wisest man who ever lived talks about how wisdom is the priority of his pursuit. Even the Psalms say "the fear of the Lord is the beginning of wisdom" (Proverbs 1:7, 9:10; Psalm 111:10). Wisdom isn't just reading the Bible. It is memorizing Scriptures. Scriptures aren't "Biblical Bumper Stickers" you slap on a situation, but instead are God's Word that becomes His will for your situation. God's word becomes embedded into who you are, into your relationship, your situations and your life. You want to find rest? Well, what does the Bible say about it? Now go and do it!

4: BE FAITHFUL...STARTING NOW.

Promotion will always call out to you. But here's a newsflash: when it does, you don't have to answer it. Because maybe God is wanting you to stay where you're at and be faithful in your current assignment. Your talents, gifts and your platform will naturally get recognition, and when it does, it will compel you to move. But you don't have to. Maybe you're not supposed to. Because opportunities are everywhere. Success is valuable but it can also be misleading. Succeeding at the wrong thing could be your biggest failure. That's why it's important to steward your "now" well because it is training and shaping for your "next." Don't take shortcuts. Shortcuts "cut short" the work of God on your life. Grow where you're planted. Grow faithfulness. Because faithfulness is one of the best evidence of success. Faithfulness is a fruit of the Spirit, and to see faithfulness in your life, you must become grounded and develop a root system.

I was out to dinner with a great friend and we were talking about how the unseen parts of our lives are so critical and rarely celebrated. We don't celebrate the prayer lives of others, we don't "anoint" our "dad diaper changes", we don't Instagram live our "quiet times" to show the world we know how to seek God, etc. What's unseen isn't as celebrated as what's on our platform. What's unseen is what's underground. And what's underground doesn't get celebrated. That's why no one walks up to a blooming rosebush that is covered in flowers and say, "that root system sure is 'purdy.'" Of course not. Most people admire the rosebush in bloom. They rarely if ever admire the root system underneath. The blossoms are what gets noticed.

The reality is: roots precede fruits. To bear great fruits you need great roots. Stay grounded. Stay focused and watch God bring your future to life. Start seeing success as less about achieving for others and more about faithfulness to others. Serving others and loving well are primary attributes of personal satisfaction and keep you grounded in all seasons so you can experience rest.

5: GROUND YOUR THEOLOGY IN JESUS.

There are many out there who will be happy to shape your theology for you. There is a lot of spiritual content on the internet. I'm not suggesting you stop growing in knowledge and in the deeper things of God. You should always be growing! I am suggesting, however, that you never go beyond the simple, child-like, overwhelming awe of who Jesus is, how He loves you and what He did for you on the cross. Center your beliefs firmly and completely around the person of Jesus Christ. Discipline your life to do as Jesus would do. Invite others to "follow you as you follow Christ" (1 Corinthians 11:1). Let the grace, truth, love and hope of Jesus guide you in all you do and your life will have a beautiful simplicity to it.

6: LET OTHERS INVEST IN YOU.

Making disciples is the mission Jesus gave us and that mission can seem daunting and tiring! But there is a relational difference between teaching a crowd on the weekend, having a Bible study in a community group and spending quality time with a few people. Jesus' model of living involved crowds, community and core. Jesus thought being devoted to a few was time well spent to make a global impact that would last generations. In the rush of trying to be everything to everyone, finding rest in being devoted to a few will simplify your faith and give you the strength to keep going. Who are you spending time with? Who you spend time with can either replenish you or deplete you. There are those who will add and multiply your life. Then there are those who will divide and subtract from your life. Surround yourself with people who make you better. We all need a group of people who you can count on to pray for you, encourage you and inspire you. If Jesus needed an "inner circle" then you do, too (Matthew 26:37).

7: STOP CHASING BALANCE.

I propose we need to be resting more and chasing less. We are conditioned to pursue an education, a career, a spouse, etc. From an early age we are conditioned to run after our goals, our dreams and our future. But running is exhausting. If you've played "tag" growing up, then you understand. We know that feeling of being "it" and chasing after those who are running away from you. If you were like me, being "it" was not always as fun as it looked. Because I wasn't the fastest. And when you have friends on the track team, it's definitely not fun. It's exhausting chasing after someone who was hard to catch.

I think balance is like that. It's hard to catch.

So many people make resolutions to find balance: balance with our family, balance with our jobs, balance with our social lives, balance with our relationships. But when has "finding balance" supposed to have been the goal?

Last time I checked, Jesus wasn't into finding balance.

Balance says that we should give equal energy and attention to everything. However, not only is this idea not possible, it's not Biblical. I believe Jesus was less about balance and more about extremes.

- He was not balanced dealing with family; Jesus chose to prioritize work over His family at times because He knew the sacredness of the moment and knew His family had to wait (Matthew 12:46–47).
- He was not balanced with work; in the midst of saving the world, He stopped and focused on His family. While dying on the cross He focused on His mother Mary because He knew what she needed at that moment and was present and available to make sure she had her needs met (John 19:26–27).
- He was not balanced with ministry; He rerouted the team when He needed to and when it didn't make sense, because He knew the true needs even when they weren't obvious (John 4:4, 27).
- He was not balanced with friends; He chose three friends as His favorites over the others, knowing that sometimes you have to be exclusive as well as inclusive (Matthew 17:1).

Jesus truly shows us how to live free from chasing balance. When He was supposed to be doing life with God or people, He was always fully present. No one has ever been more passionate about people than Jesus. However, He didn't just react to the whims of the people, the needs of the community, the urgency of the ministry.

He responded to the need of God in all of His situations (John 4:34). Jesus seemed to be more concerned about doing everything with God, rather than making God one priority among many other priorities. Jesus chose to make God the center of everything. He made his life and ministry less about prioritization and more about assimilation.

We've been conditioned to operate from the prioritization of first God, then family, then work, then church, … etc. Again, that's prioritization. However, Jesus operated from assimilation. Jesus chose God and family, God and work, God and church, God and … etc. Think of it in music terms. Rather than God being a primary note in the song, God is the harmony, bringing all the other parts together. The Bible makes it clear that whatever we choose to do, it's about harmonizing everything with God's will. Colossians 3:17, 23–24 shows us this:

> Whatever you do, whether in word or deed, do it all in the name of the Lord Jesus, giving thanks to God the Father through Him. Again, whatever we do, in work or business, it is to be done in the name of Jesus, with integrity and a sense of Christian service. … Whatever you do, work at it with all your heart, as working for the Lord, not for human masters, since you know that you will receive an inheritance from the Lord as a reward. It is the Lord Christ you are serving.

All that we do is done with Christ as the focus. So I am proposing that instead of finding balance, let's find rhythm.

Rhythms naturally have rest built into it or it wouldn't be a rhythm ... it would simply be a pounding note that never stops. It's the "rest" in the beats that gives it rhythm. For rhythm to work it must have movement AND rest.

My point is this: instead of shuffling between competing loyalties that must constantly be balanced, what if we saw them as a complimentary rhythm. When we stop living from "Jesus then..." and start living from "Jesus and...." our life simplifies into one simple pursuit of Christ. Because when I make Jesus my focus, then Jesus gets my attention AND my family, work, ministry, etc. They all automatically get my affection all at once because Jesus permeates it all. Stop chasing balance, and start to find your rhythm.

8: MANAGE YOURSELF.

We all have 24 hours in a day. Yet it feels as though some of us have "many more" hours in a day than others. There are those who seem to always get their to-do lists done. We have to learn to manage ourselves first before we can effectively manage those around us. Whether we are a parent, a spouse, a team leader at work, the person leading the organization or the church, we have to manage self. This will always be our most difficult person to manage. If you lead yourself correctly, others will trust you and follow you. If you lead yourself poorly, you'll eventually lose the people you need the most and lose yourself! That's why learning the skill of how to manage yourself will be one of the greatest gifts you can give to yourself and those around you.

We all have the same amount of time given to us every day. Your deliberate use of the time everyone else wastes, will give you the privilege of finding the rhythm everyone else wants. Being aware of our 24 hours and how we manage it is important to us and God. Psalms confirms this:

"Teach us to number our days that we may gain a heart of wisdom"(Psalm 90:12).

God instructs us that counting the days (even hours and minutes) gives us the wisdom we need to live the life we were made to have. The request by God to number our days means that we need God to reveal to us the limited time of life. When we understand this it will help us to become wiser and help us to make better choices on how we live this life we've been given.

Here are some quick hitters to get you going on learning to prioritize your day.

1: REALIZE WHAT YOU THINK IS IMPORTANT MAY NOT BE THAT IMPORTANT.

There are many things that want our attention. There are many voices that shout at us to give them attention. So our focus becomes divided. The demands of others can paralyze us. Just like a lion in a three-ring circus sees the man in front of him, but once the chair is placed in front of him this "killing machine" becomes a paralyzed cat unable to even focus on the four legs not to mention the man holding the chair (that's why the lion-tamer has a chair; weird, but I get it now), we too can allow the wrong thing to take our attention and focus. Instead, focus on one thing at a time and watch your "to-do list" become a "done-and-done list." God makes that easy by reminding us this simple principle in prioritizing, "Seek first the Kingdom and all these things will be added to you" (Matthew 6:33).

2: WORK SMARTER NOT HARDER.

I don't know who started that phrase but I've heard that in all my leadership circles. Being more intense at what you need to do doesn't magically give you more time. But being more insightful at what you need to do helps you find a better way, making the most of what you have. Prioritize the time to discover new app's for better productivity. Find others that you trust to help be a "second set of hands" to work on "that" while you do "this." Devote yourself to finding a solution for the problem instead of drifting into maintenance of the problem.

3: CREATE "WHITE SPACE" IN YOUR LIFE.

In design, "white space" is negative space. It's not blank space because it has a purpose. It is balancing the rest of the design by bringing what is on the page into greater view. The white space helps focus your visual attention. We need white space in our daily lives just as much as we need it in design because it reveals if our lives are over-cluttered and over-booked, and therefore we can't prioritize. Time scarcity is like kryptonite for productivity. We need to build margin into our calendar because a lot of activity does not mean a lot of accomplishments. The greater the responsibilities, the greater the need for "white space" in your day.

4: STOP MAKING EVERYTHING A PRIORITY BECAUSE THEN NOTHING BECOMES PRIORITY.

When you say everything has high priority, then everything will have inferiority. When you make everything a priority you ultimately make nothing a priority. If you do this, you have a hard time making decisions. When you are unable and unwilling to make any decisions, you won't get anything done. Not only does your list continue to get longer and longer but it also makes you unstable:

> For the ambivalent person believes one minute and doubts the next. Being undecided makes you become like the rough seas driven and tossed by the wind. You're up one minute and tossed down the next. When you are half-hearted and wavering it leaves you unstable (James 1:6-8 TPT).

Make a list of the things that you need to do. Then put a number by the one's that are most important for you to get done for that day. Once you identify the list of top tasks, order them appropriately. Make it a goal for that day to accomplish those top three tasks that day. Add more tasks as they arrive to tomorrow's list and repeat the exercise again.

5: RESIST "YOUR GOOD" SABOTAGING "YOUR BEST."

It's easy to prioritize the good decisions from the bad. For example, "Do I binge another season of Shark Tank, or do I finally paint over our purple bathroom the color grey that Joanna Gaines swears by which the wife bought for me that has been sitting in our storage room for two weeks?" Binging a TV show when the wife has a project list for you to do probably doesn't classify at the level of "good" and is one step lower to "bad" decision. Obviously, the real challenge is prioritizing the good decisions from the great decisions. They can look similar but will have a different result. Take time to discover what is the best use of your time as you prioritize your life.

6: CHOOSE TO BE PROACTIVE NOT REACTIVE.

Being proactive means "I have things to do." Being reactive means, "I have to do things." If you have the characteristics of a proactive person, that means you are preparing, planning, anticipating, and are responsible and effective in your day to day life. If you have the characteristics of a reactive person, this means you are repairing instead of preparing. A reactive person is preventing instead of planning. Also, they are putting requests of others in the calendar instead of putting their responsibilities toward others in the calendars. Ultimately they are reactive instead of effective.

7: "PARETO YOURSELF" BEFORE YOU WRECK YOURSELF.

The "Pareto Principle" is a familiar concept to many of us. It is named after Italian economist Vilfredo Pareto and is more commonly known as the 80/20 principle. Applying this principle simply means that spending 20 percent of your time and energy on your priorities will give you 80 percent return on your productivity. Simply put, discover and categorize the top 20% of your to-do list and you will get an 80% return. How's that for day's work?

CHAPTER 3 QUESTIONS

1. What does Sabbath mean to you?

2. Have you ever had a spiritual meltdown because you've been neglecting rest?

3. How does seeing rest as a command and not a suggestion change you?

4. It's easy to let your fire go out. So what keeps your fire going?

5. How has hurry been the enemy of your spiritual life?

6. Has disappointment caused you to find a lack of peace and rest? Why or why not?

7. How could not chasing balance but finding rhythm change your life?

8. Are you being more proactive or more reactive in your life lately?

4

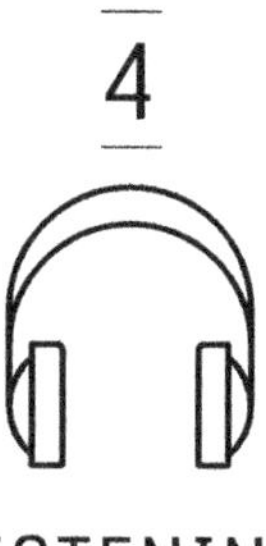

LISTENING

VALUING CONVICTIONS OVER OPINIONS

As Christians we battle between faith and feelings, authority and apathy, obedience and convenience. One particular contrast that is notable in most of us as Christians is the battle of conviction versus opinion. Convictions are part of the Christian life. Jesus came to bring conviction to help us live and love as His followers (John 16:8). Opinions are also part of our human experience. All the information we receive daily produces so many opinions about so many things. Learning to differentiate between conviction and opinion is important.

Conviction is defined as a "strong persuasion or belief." It's the state of being "convinced." It comes from the Latin word translated "to conquer." Contrast that to opinions. Webster's Dictionary says opinions "lack certainty." Opinions are the scrawny guys in the gladiator ring of the mind. They aren't sure of their victory, have minimal weaponry, and have no grit for the fight.

Think of the character Korg from the movie Thor: Ragnarok who said:

> I'm kind of like the leader in here. I'm made of rocks, as you can see. But don't let that intimidate you. You don't need to be afraid ... I tried to start a revolution ... but I didn't print enough pamphlets so hardly anyone turned up. Except for my mum and her boyfriend.

Opinions are the "Korgs" in your brain. They talk a tough game, but in the end they are not as strong as you think. But convictions are conquering warriors in your brain. They have the weapons, the strength, and the power to win the battle of the mind and to help you make the decisions necessary for your life to align with the life of Jesus.

Conviction gives you the strength to accomplish the impossible regardless of what others think. Think of conviction as the muscle tissue of your beliefs. The more you listen to it and flex it, the stronger you get. Every fiber of your being is in alignment to the movement of your beliefs. When conviction flexes its muscle, it gives you the power to overcome the opinions of those around you. We give opinions more power than what they are worth. When someone gives you their opinion on something, we tend to take it seriously. And while the source of the opinion matters in regards to its credibility and validity, our human side of us seems to give it more strength than it really has. We allow those opinionated words to continue to echo in our heads. We hear them when we are alone, when we are at work, in our relationships and when we go to sleep at night.

Opinions seem to have all this power over us.

While it may seem that opinions are strong, your convictions are stronger. Your convictions are ultimately more powerful than opinions. Even though you can't actually "see" conviction, it does reveal the virtues and values that you have. Your beliefs, your character and your standards will ultimately lead you, drive you and you will carry them with you wherever you go. It is the evidence of what you believe.

In contrast, opinion is the evidence of what others believe. Opinions are a belief or a judgment that is supported by "insufficient certainty." That's like saying, "I will never not believe you sometimes." The only thing certain is opinions cannot ALWAYS be trusted. Because opinions are someone else's interpretation, perspective and meaning of a situation. While not every opinion is wrong, it's still someone else's point of view. Yet, God's interpretation, perspective and meaning of a situation can always be trusted and is the most accurate. Conviction is God's interpretation of a word, a meaning or a scenario. Through the Holy Spirit (John 16:8), God helps you get an accurate perspective and gain understanding in all areas of your life. This is why leaning on your convictions is so powerful.

Convictions empower you to resist what others say about you and embrace what God says about you. Convictions compel you to trust yourself less and trust God more. Conviction transforms you from having a good idea to becoming a good example for others to follow. No matter where you find yourself in life, what changes the people and the world around you is your example and not your opinion.

A disciple chooses to build their life on convictions instead of opinions.

So how do you tell the difference between convictions and opinions?

1: OPINIONS FUEL CONDEMNATION BUT CONVICTIONS FUEL GUIDANCE.

That's the difference between condemnation and conviction. Condemnation and shame will always tell you who you aren't. Conviction will always tell you who you are. That's why shame is a "counterfeit conviction." Shame tells you that you aren't enough, but Jesus always reminds us that He is enough. Shame says you are a bad person and attacks your identity and God's identity. But conviction reminds you that you are still a child of God and that God is good.

The Bible says that you are child of God with a good Father. This is always the starting point for Christians and their identity. We know this from the Bible, which gives us the conviction that this is true, "But to all who did receive him, who believed in his name, he gave the right to become children of God" (John 1:12).

God is identified as our Father 265 times in Scripture. Most of those are found in the New Testament because through Christ, we have a new identity as an adopted child of God (Romans 8:15). As Christians we can trust this confirmation of our identity and live out this conviction. Conviction will confirm your identity while opinion can confuse your identity. For example, we have heard people give this opinion:

"If God loves you, He wouldn't have let that bad thing happen to you."

Opinions give you uncertainty about who God is and who you are. They make you uncertain about God's identity as a Good Father and your identity as His child. Your identity should never depend on the opinion of another person alone. That's why social media comments, popularity, etc. are not reliable or sustainable. I love that Mary (Martha's sister) chose the one thing that couldn't be taken from her, and that was her connection to Jesus.

"But only one thing is necessary. Mary has chosen the good portion, and it will not be taken away from her" (Luke 10:42).

Choose to attach your identity to something that cannot be taken away. Connect your identity to something (your faith, your cause, your family, etc.) that can't be stolen by others.

2: OPINIONS CAUSE YOU TO DRIFT AND CONVICTIONS ANCHOR YOU TO TRUTH.

Opinions change on a whim and if you change with them, people will begin to lose their trust in you. They'll never know where you stand. That's the great thing about convictions. They tell others what you believe and what you won't tolerate.

However if you change your convictions based on other's opinions, you will have a harder time standing firm.

Doubts will flood in and you will have a difficult time making the hard choices in life.

Opinions will compel you to seek answers from others, not because you're looking for the right path, but because you want the approval.

In contrast convictions keep you on the the right path. They are like those bumps on the road when you are on a long road trip. I love road trips with my family. We make my playlists, we have our favorite "car games" ready and we have plenty of jerky and licorice. While our road trips always have a strong start, they sometimes have us crawling over the finish line. Our excitement for the journey had us singing, laughing and eating in the beginning. But somewhere along the way, our excitement of traveling to our favorite place took a turn. Because now the food is gone, the playlist has been played, the car games are worn out and the landscape all begins to look and feel the same. They're all sleeping and now it's just me staring at miles of road. It's part of being a dad. Making sure the family gets there safely. But that doesn't mean that I'm still not getting bored, fatigued and even sleepy. When the journey is long, the scenery is dull and the destination is nowhere in sight...that's when I am prone to drift. In the midst of my monotony, I hear that sound of the rumble on the shoulder of the road:

"VRR-VRR! VRR-VRR!"
"VRR-VRR! VRR-VRR!"

If you've driven for any amount of time on the freeway, you will recognize that sound. It's the sound of drifting off the road into the shoulder and slowly veering towards the ditch. My eyes that were heavier than usual pop open as I steer the car back on to the road again. I adjust my mirror, change the music, and check my GPS for the nearest gas station for a Red Bull. The VRR-VRR got my attention!

Convictions are the "VRR-VRR" in your inner man from the Holy Spirit. They are meant to catch your attention and wake you up to where you are at and remind you to stop drifting. As you are following Jesus you are prone to drift. Hebrews 2:1 says,

"So we must listen very carefully to the truth we have heard, or we may drift...."

Convictions keep you from drifting and help you take notice of what is being said, heard, read and believed. They compel you to adjust your thoughts, insights and beliefs back onto the narrow road of faith that's found in Jesus.

3: YOU CAN FOLLOW PEOPLE'S OPINIONS OR YOU CAN FOLLOW GOD'S DIRECTION.

It should be noted that while many people give us their opinions, not all opinions are bad and should be ignored. There are opinions that are spoken into us that are in alignment with God's Word and God's will for us. These opinions are inspired by God to encourage us, challenge us and help us to understand who we are and what God is doing. Our family and friends will give us their opinions and these words should affirm who God is and what God is already doing in specific areas of our lives. Almost as if God is giving His wisdom, His counsel and His understanding through our family, friends, co-workers. etc. These words that are being spoken can be defined as opinions, but their shape changes and they cease becoming opinions and transform into wisdom, correction and encouragement from God. You will always confront opinions that are not in alignment with God's plans and purpose for your life and those should be ignored. But the opinions that are congruent with God's will for your life become God's voice into your life to inspire you and give you courage to keep going.

Convictions will make you courageous to follow God's direction for your life while opinions can make you complacent. A courageous person is very different than a complacent person. When you are complacent, you can become sedated enough to miss opportunities right in front of you. Opinions can make you digress but convictions always help you to make progress. Don't let other people's opinions chip away at your confidence. The New Young Christian must do their best not to be ruled by what other people think, but instead by what God thinks. You'll get opinions from everyone, but the opinions of others are no match for the mind of Christ in you. That mind comes from confiding in God, and trusting Him with your calling and your future.

The reality is getting one hundred opinions from others of how great you are to "build your confidence" doesn't compare to the weight of God's opinion of who you are. It's easy to allow our confidence to be subdued because of the opinions of others. But your confidence is one of the greatest gifts from God that you can possess. It helps you to face your fears, take risks and overcome obstacles. Not only that it moves you closer to God. God says it this way, "Let us then draw near with confidence to the throne of grace" (Hebrews 4:16).

Drawing near to God requires confidence. And this holy confidence comes from the understanding that we are loved by Jesus. Jesus love for us is not earned but initiated by God (1 John 4:19). This gives us wonderful confidence to draw nearer to God. And the closer you are to God, the more confident you get. Because it's here that you can differentiate between the wrong things others say about you and the right things God says about you. Because the closer you are to God, the easier it is to hear God's voice. There is a correlation between your convictions as a Christian and your ability to hear God's voice for your life.

The best way we can drown out opinions and live from conviction is to listen to God's voice. I have heard other Christians say this: "Why does God speak to others but not to me?" The reality is that it's simply not true. God actually does want to speak to you and is speaking to you. He has so many things to say and reveal about His thoughts toward you that they are as many as the grains of sand on the beach (Psalm 139:17–18). So if God has that many things to say about you, maybe we should figure out how to tune in. Any time someone who loves you more than you can ever imagine wants to speak to you, you should want to hear what they have to say.

I have made it a personal mission to try to hear God because God's voice and my convictions cannot be separated. The closer you get to God, the better you can hear Him. The more you know God, the more you know yourself. The opposite is true as well! The less you know God, the less you know about yourself.

Here's what we know about God's voice:

- God has a voice. We know this because of the third verse of the Bible, when God spoke light into darkness (Genesis 1:3).
- You can hear His voice if you are a follower of Jesus. Jesus said these powerful words: "I am the good shepherd and I know My own and My own know Me. My sheep hear My voice and I know them and they follow Me" (John 10:14, 27).
- You hear by the Holy Spirit. Jesus sent the Holy Spirit to guide us into truth, to speak these truths loud and clear (John 14:26; 16:13–15).
- Hearing God is prophetic. Prophecy starts with Jesus, is about Jesus and restores people back to Jesus (Revelation 19:10)

I want to be a Christian who is with Jesus so that I can hear Him and be with Him. Out of that intimacy comes a revelation of who He is, who I am and what I am made to do. If we can cultivate that kind of closeness with God, it allows us to see and hear things that will overflow out of us.

The love of God leads me to have a prophetic lifestyle, or in other words, a lifestyle of conviction that lives from hearing God speak, not from my opinions or those of others . That's why Paul says, "Follow the way of love and eagerly desire the gifts of the Spirit, especially prophecy" (1 Corinthians 14:1). Prophetic words and hearing the voice of God will always affirm who you are and confirm who you were always meant to be. When God speaks to you, He connects you to your designed purpose, what you were created to be and do. When you obey your convictions, you catch a glimpse of the "you" that you were always meant to be.

So, how do we hear God's voice?
Here are 5 truths that will help you to
hear God more clearly in your life.

1: GOD SPEAKS TO EVERYONE.

We live in a noisy culture. We also have a God who speaks regularly. He is speaking "Come to me," to those who don't yet know Him. And to those who do know Him, He is saying "I am here." God is always revealing who He is and who you are supposed to be (see Romans 5:8, 10:17). So be still and know Him (Psalm 46:10). The Hebrew word for "know" means to "be intimately acquainted with." So start spending intentional time simply listening.

We do a lot of "asking God to ___" and not enough of "hearing God say ___."

My friend Eric Samuel Timm says this in his book 'The Static Jedi': "Battling the noise is creating a space for God and acknowledging the space He occupies, which is all of it. Invite God into all 24 hours of your day." Make space for God to speak. God speaks to everyone. He is speaking to you. So invite Him in and hear what He has to say.

2: GOD'S VOICE IS RECOGNIZED BY HIS LOVING TONE.

God's voice sounds like love (Galatians 5:6). There is no condemnation in Christ, but there is grace and mercy. When you hear "grace and mercy" you are hearing God because that's what He sounds like. These two themes are strong indicators that what you are hearing is God's voice. Grace is acceptance by God that you cannot earn, and mercy is forgiveness that you don't deserve but have received in Christ. It is faith expressing itself with love.

3: GOD'S PURPOSE FOR SPEAKING TO YOU AND TO OTHERS IS PRIMARILY TO REVEAL HIS LOVE.

Jesus longed for the disciples to experience the love of the Father. The love of the Father that was essential for Jesus to live by is the same love that Jesus wants us to experience and that is available for us (John 17:24–25). Jesus didn't do anything without the Father's permission. What if we lived the same way? When you are experiencing the true love of God, you experience the conviction of God to love others just the same.

4: GOD REVEALS HIS THOUGHTS TO YOU SO THAT YOU CAN UNDERSTAND HIM.

You become transformed when your mind is renewed by God's thoughts (Romans 12:2). You hear God by the Holy Spirit. No one knows the thoughts of God except the Spirit of God. Through the Spirit, God allows us to see and know his will, purpose and plans (1 Corinthians 2:9). The thoughts that He has are many for you (Psalm 139: 17-18). As many as the grains of sand on the seashore. What if you could grab one "grain of thought" that God has about you? How would that change your life?

5: GOD'S VOICE MAKES YOU COMPLETE.

The heart of the disciples who experienced the presence and life-giving words of Jesus was to bring that same experience to others. Experiencing the voice of the Father makes you complete not only relationally, but spiritually (1 John 1:1–4).

Adam and Eve lived complete in the presence of God daily. They loved God and heard from Him regularly in the garden of Eden. They both heard God the clearest before they both fell from grace. It was in the garden where man faced the first battle of opinion versus conviction. Adam heard from God to "cultivate the garden and to keep it."

> The Lord God commanded the man saying, 'From any tree of the garden you may eat freely; but from the tree of the knowledge of good and evil you shall not eat, for in the day that you eat from it you will surely die' (Genesis 2:15-17).

Eat freely. A clear directive and felt conviction from God for Adam and Eve. Seems simple enough. Who doesn't love to eat freely. That vocal command is a conviction I can follow. Eating freely is my vacation. That's our Thanksgiving in the Pastian household. That's birthday week for everyone in my family. That's Olive Garden on all-you-can-eat pasta night. The conviction to "eat freely" doesn't bother me because I have a pretty solid "dad bod" right now (don't worry I'm working on it...kind of). But these were life-giving words to Adam and Eve who were given permission to be in the garden and enjoy the relationship of their Creator and the fruit of their labor. "Eat freely" was the conviction from God to mankind to enjoy each other in the garden.

But there was only one rule in the garden of Eden "don't eat from the tree." Because love is a choice and never forced. Obeying that single conviction would lead mankind to choose God and to choose love. Because God's love leads to God's relationship with us.

Choosing God like this is what the Bible calls holiness, and holiness forms the "bedrock" to our convictions. Holiness is a word that has gotten a bad rap in the church. So what if you defined holiness as "protecting what is most valuable, sacred, and special by keeping it safe, secure, and protected." That is your relationship with God! As Christians we choose to align our convictions with God and fight against the opinions that could hurt our relationship with God. The very words of Satan in the Garden is the first time Adam and Eve are confronted with an opinion:

> Now the serpent was more crafty than any of the wild animals the Lord God had made. He said to the woman, "Did God really say, 'You must not eat from any tree in the garden?'"
>
> The woman said to the serpent, "We may eat fruit from the trees in the garden, but God did say, 'You must not eat fruit from the tree that is in the middle of the garden, and you must not touch it, or you will die.'"
>
> 'You will not certainly die,' the serpent said to the woman (Genesis 3:1-4).

"Did God really say?" This is the first time the truth of "what God said" is confronted by the opinion of "what they said." This is the reality of everyday life for the believer. We are confronted with a choice to obey God's conviction about something or "their" opinion about something. The choice that we make in those moments will either help or hurt our relationship. So we make a choice to fiercely protect and nurture our relationship with God. It's saying a simple "yes" to God in everything He brings you and not filing through a complicated list of "no's" about everything around you. It's embracing who you are with God rather than resisting who you are without God. Holiness proves who God is and who you are.

Holiness is being set apart so that you can go back into the crowds with a conviction to affect the opinions of others. Holiness is influence. David was set apart in a field and set apart by Samuel so that he could go into the crowds of soldiers and influence a king, an army, and a giant. Moses was set apart in the wilderness to go back into the culture of Egypt to change the hearts of an administration of oppression. Jesus was set apart in a desert so He could go back and face the opposition. Holiness doesn't keep us separated but compels us to run towards our devils, our Pharisees, our giants and our Pharaoh's. The more holy we are, the more convictions we carry; and those convictions will conquer opinions when necessary and compel us to live our lives more fully!

QUESTIONS FOR CHAPTER 4

1. When was a time someone's opinion impacted your life?

2. How can being a good example inspire someone more than giving your opinion?

3. How have you seen opinions confuse your identity or convictions confirm your identity?

4. How does hearing God's voice strengthen your convictions?

5. Does the word "holiness" give you more inspiration to run after God or run away from the world?
Why or why not?

5

CONQUERING

STOPPING UNSTOPPABLE SINS

When I was little I flushed a lot of things down the toilet. There were many times I would rip toilet paper and make them into small boats that would meet their imminent doom. I would pretend that ominous swirl was a "whirlpool of death" that would devour toilet paper boats, popsicle sticks, my green army men, an action figure or two, hot wheel cars...never to be seen again.

Unless it was too big.

Then I had a choice to either force-feed this porcelain monster a second time or dry my tortured items off for future play (and you thought Sid from Toy Story was bad). Sometimes my Mom would come in and find some of these fun items floating lifelessly in this germ-saturated abyss. I guess what I thought was gone forever had a way of not staying gone for long.

I wish when you repented of a particular sin, it was gone forever. Never to return. Just like the toilet swirl in my bathroom. But unfortunately sin has a way of not staying away for long.

When you repent, Jesus does remove your sin as far as the east is from the west (Psalm 103:12). But for some sins, when you think it's gone, you find it floating back up to the surface again. You find yourself dealing with the same sin yet again. Repentance is normal for a Christian. But after a few days, weeks or months you are suddenly faced with that reality that some sins are harder to get rid of than others.

Why is that?

Well, let's unpack sin for a moment. Everyone sins. Sin doesn't just affect Christians, it affects the entire human race (Romans 3:23). While sin affects everyone, not everyone knows its effect. The world around us leans into "self-help" books and while all these aren't bad, they won't actually solve the problem of sin in our lives unless we identify sin for what it is. The Bible describes sin as a ruthless, defiant force in our lives:

- Sin deceives you (Genesis 3:13).
- Sin desires you (Genesis 4:7).
- Sin destroys you (Genesis 6:7).
- Sin wages war over you (Romans 7:23).
- Sin entices you (James 1:14).
- Sin entangles you (Hebrews 12:1).

Sin damaged all of us and continues to wreak havoc in our lives since the beginning. Sin has a way of being persistent. And unstoppable. Many of us struggle with those seemingly "unstoppable sins," those entrenched, difficult-to-dislodge sins that continually bug us as we do our best to follow Christ. The gospel gives us hope that ALL sin, even our unstoppable sins, can be both forgiven and subdued. But because sin has such persistence and power, we have got to be vigilant in our struggle against it. Since sin is so vicious (the Bible literally says the result of sin is death—Romans 6:23) then why would we expect such a comfortable and easy battle with it? If sin's purpose is to fight us to the death then we have to have the same tenacity to fight sin to the death.

Fighting something to the death is not easy and extremely brutal. The Roman gladiator is one such fighter that had the strength and persistent spirit to fight to the death. Called 'gladiator' because of their unique short swords called the "gladius", these slaves and prisoners were sent to large arenas to fight to the death. The thirty, forty, or even fifty thousand spectators from all sections of Roman society flocked to be entertained by gory spectacles. Encapsulating Roman virtues of honor and courage, these gladiators showed their skills as citizens of Rome by fighting beasts and barbarians in a killed or be killed contest (it is also to be noted that until their outlaw by Sptimius Severus in 200 CE, women were permitted to fight as gladiators). God even uses such imagery to inspire us to fight as He calls us "citizens of heaven" (Philippians 3:20) wearing the "full armor of God" (Ephesians 6:10) as we fight as "slaves to God" (Romans 6:22), battling for our personal victory over sin. The fight we are in has hope. The truth is our hope is in Jesus.

What we think of as unbeatable or unstoppable is beatable and stoppable because of Christ's work on the cross which was unbeatable and is still unstoppable (1 John 1:9).

So why do some sins persist and harass us after we confess?

Let's break this down. There are 3 parts to how we are made as human beings. We have a body, soul and spirit. This is true according to the Bible:

"Now may the God of peace make you holy in every way and may your whole spirit and soul and body be kept blameless until our Lord Jesus Christ comes again" (1 Thessalonians 5:23).

First, your spirit is your connection to God. It's your ability to receive from and connect with God. It's the part of you that speaks to God. It's the part of you that hears from God (Psalm 104:29, James 2:26, Ecclesiastes 12:7).

The second part of 'you' is your soul. Your soul is different and it's uniquely separated from your spirit. Even the Bible talks about the soul and spirit being distinctly different pieces of your spiritual design (Hebrews 4:12). Your soul is basically who you are—your mind, your emotion, and your will. It's you being you in the world. But the function of your soul is to express God. Mary did this when her "soul magnified the Lord" (Luke 1:46-47).

Finally, your body. Your body is just that. It's your physical body. Not much to explain here other than God made you, and He made you unique (Psalm 139). You have unique responsibility to express yourself in the world and express God to the world.

We are a spirit being, we live in a body, and we possess a soul. Period. All three work together to make you, 'you'. This "trinitarian" make-up of who you are is important, especially when it comes to your salvation experience.

Here's what happens at salvation...

First, at salvation your spirit is made new. In some way that we can't see, your spirit is redeemed and your connection to God is restored. When you confess with your mouth and believe in your heart that Jesus Christ is Lord, you become born again. Your spirit becomes pure and it begins a constant and unbreakable communion with God that can never be impure again (2 Corinthians 5:17, Romans 6:2-6; Ezekiel 36:26, 11:19). This is restoring you back to God's original plan in the Garden of Eden when mankind and God had an unbreakable connection. Your salvation experience restores that connection and nothing can get in between that connection. As a matter of fact, God clearly states that nothing can ever separate you from this connection you have through Jesus (Romans 8:31-39). This new relationship is how you connect and relate to our Creator, God.

Second, at salvation, your soul begins transformation. It isn't instant like your spirit but it is in a process of metamorphosis. Romans 12:2 helps us understand that we are "not to be conformed to this world but transformed." Just like there are not "instant butterflies" but a transformation that takes the caterpillar from ground to flight. The same is with our soul. There is a transformation that takes place over time. In other words, the day after your salvation, you will still have a bad thought, make bad choices, and have a "bad bent" towards certain things. As your spirit is connecting to God and you are hearing Him speak and direct your life, your mind begins to think more like Christ, you become more aware of your sinful issues, and start living a better self-controlled life. The choices you get to make every day now become better, smarter, and spiritually healthier. For example, you want to start reading the Bible, you long for your next church service, you begin to pray more, you start singing worship songs on your own because you long for the presence of God, you start thinking differently than you thought before about the choices you are making, your relationships, your career, your future, etc.

While your SPIRIT and your SOUL are experiencing the wonderful effects of your salvation experience, your BODY is still experiencing the effects of sin. You will still get a cold, get sick, experience sickness and disease. Your body doesn't become perfect. You may receive a miracle from God and get healed at your salvation experience. While that is not a guarantee, it can happen and has happened with some Christians. But the good news is whatever happens your bodily breakdowns can become a prayer moment for you to draw closer to God and an opportunity for you to experience supernatural power of healing in your body.

The Bible is also clear that when we all die one day, we receive new bodies that will never break down and will never experience sickness and disease ever again (Romans 8:23).

Now that we are understanding how all of these areas work independently, how do these 3 areas work in relation to each other throughout your Christian life?

First, your spirit continues to connect, give and receive from God through daily Bible reading, prayer, worship, etc. You begin to hear God's voice more and you begin to have greater revelation on the plans and purposes for your life. Second, your soul is being transformed day by day to be more like Christ. You begin to change the way you think about others, how you see your job, how you lead your family, etc. Your soul (mind, will and emotions) are being refined daily as you spend time in His presence, as you learn to think like Him and behave like Him and love like Him (1 Peter 1:22-23, Romans 12:1-2). Over your lifetime as you get closer to God, your bad thoughts, negative emotions and unhealthy choices will become less and less as you love God daily. You will notice this change in your soul as you are reading the Bible more and more, you crave worship, you long to serve and bless others more than you have before. And at the end of your life, when you finally arrive in heaven, your soul becomes perfect and you will fully be alive as you see and experience the true and unhindered revelation of Christ. Third, your body will continue to decay because of sin. Sickness and disease will continue to affect us and our world. But we will experience miracles along the way and healings along the way. God will restore, preserve and sustain you along your faith journey through prayer times and unique miraculous moments where God does a restorative miracle. We can experience heaven on earth with our bodies when God chooses to heal our bodies but our complete healing comes in heaven. You won't receive your new body until heaven and that's when it becomes brand new just like your spirit and soul, never to experience the decay of sin ever again. It's not until we finally get to heaven that we are promised a new body that will be congruent with our new spirit and purified soul (1 Corinthians 15:54-57).

So what about that unbeatable sin?

That unbeatable sin seems unbeatable because your soul—the part of you that helps you make the willful choices to align with Jesus - knows and believes you need Jesus. But your soul is caught in a tug of war. You know you need to choose God, but you crave the old pleasures of that old life that you gave to Jesus when you "died to self" (Galatians 2:20). So in a moment of weakness, you "give in" and choose wrong. Your spirit that is connected to God knows this and you sense and feel the conviction of the sin. Your soul feels that guilty conviction that your choice was wrong. And your body experiences the effect of that choice, too.

While your spirit is fully transformed by Jesus at salvation, your soul is not fully transformed in this area of sin. It will come over time, but it isn't instant. So you are in the tension of "what I want to do I do not do, but what I hate I do" (Romans 7:15) because your spirit is fighting with your soul. You know what to do because your spirit is willing but your flesh is weak (Matthew 26:41).

I know those moments well when it comes to being a dad and watching movies with my kiddos. I have teenagers, and while I'm young at heart, I do feel my age at times.

Case in point: I was introducing my kids to The Lord of the Rings Trilogy. We have all three movies and we don't mess around. We buy the directors cut versions of all our movies because I want the full experience. So when I say "let's watch Lord of the Rings", I am meaning "clear your calendars kids, because we are now part of something that will be lasting for hours". While I've declared a 7:30pm start time, for some reason my kids don't officially get downstairs to our movie room for another hour or two. Which means, I'm watching this movie till midnight. Even though we are starting an hour or two late, I'm feeling good, the popcorn is ready, and I'm locked and loaded for watching Frodo make his way from the shire while I get to be "dorky dad" telling my kids how I was in Oxford visiting the very places where J.R.R. Tolkien had walked. But just like in my 5K Turkey Trot at Thanksgiving, I start out of the gate strong only to find myself getting passed up by more experienced running enthusiasts and I barely make it over the finish line as my enthusiasm drifts and in this case I also drift…off to sleep! That's what Dad life will do to you. My spirit (and my kids) wanted Frodo and Lord of the Rings but my flesh wanted to be "lord of the pillow!" My spirit was willing but my flesh was weak and my body said, "goodnight."

My point is, you will have weak moments. You will not be perfect as a Christian and you will screw up from time to time. You will have good intentions but will drift off and miss the mark. This doesn't mean you don't love God or that your salvation isn't secure. It just means there is a part of your life that is unfinished where God is still working out your salvation (Philippians 2:12). This incongruent moment when you love God but are longing for sin is when sin appears unstoppable. It seems unstoppable because you've prayed and ask God to forgive you but you still long for it and in some cases still engage in it. You keep doing the things you don't want to do and the things you don't want to do, you do! The Bible speaks about this in Romans 7:21-25:

> Although I want to do good, evil is right there with me. For in my inner being I delight in God's law; but I see another law at work in me, waging war against the law of my mind and making me a prisoner of the law of sin at work within me. What a wretched man I am! Who will rescue me from this body that is subject to death? Thanks be to God, who delivers me through Jesus Christ our Lord!

God understands. God gets it.
But it still is emotionally and spiritually draining.
Here's the good news...

You can stop an unstoppable sin by practicing these four spiritual postures towards sin:

1: HATE IT.

A pure hatred for what this sin is, is doing and is going to do is a good starting point. The emotion of hate is powerful when in the right context. When we bring Christ into the context of our sin we feel the need to be saved from it. In the case of unstoppable sins, when we bring our sin into the context of Christ we feel the need to hate it.

Psalm 97:10 says, "You who love the Lord, hate evil. He protect the lives of His godly people and rescues them."

When you hate something, you are gripped with an emotion that is powerful. So channel that emotion towards the power of sin. Fight power with power. We have to feel the magnitude of our sin and be gripped by its stench and repulsed by its actions. Sin turns healthy marriages into abusive relationships. Sin turns good men into addicts. Sin takes confident women and makes them insecure. Sin takes trusted friends and turns them into hated enemies. If we pass over sin lightly with shallow applications of grace and flippant prayers of forgiveness—we will probably never get around to the serious vigilance required for killing it. Truly subduing sin requires properly resisting it.

So, take a moment to stop and examine for a second that particular sin that you just can't seem to beat. Really look at it, what it can do to you, and how it will affect your relationship with God and your relationships with others. For example, if you can't stop being offended, sin's most corrupt end-result of living offended will be loneliness. If you can't stop looking at porn, sin's most corrupt end-result will be a miserable and unfulfilled relationship that could end badly. So get mad, get angry and hate it...hate the sin that clearly hates you!

In Surprised by Joy, C.S. Lewis says that "the surest means of disarming an anger or a lust (is) to turn your attention from the girl or the insult and start examining the passion itself." Stopping unstoppable sins often requires this uncomfortable, honest reflection and acknowledgement about what the sin is doing within us.

2: STARVE IT.

I remember seeing the film A Beautiful Mind. In this film, Russell Crowe plays Nash, a brilliant mathematician who came up with the game theory of economics and won the Nobel Prize, decades later, in 1994. At age 31, he develops schizophrenia and suffers a mental breakdown. Imagine being diagnosed with schizophrenia and being told that several of your friends are actually not real. He genuinely misses talking to them. So how does he deal with this battle of the mind? ... he simply chooses to ignore them.

He says this in the film, "I just choose not to acknowledge them. Like a diet of the mind, I just choose not to indulge certain appetites."

Even at the end of his life he still sees the delusions, but they have lost their destructive power over him. In the same way, what if you chose to put your mind on a diet? Choose today to not indulge. Choose today to not even acknowledge your sinful desires - starve them of your affections and your attention, and they grow weaker. The more we indulge in our sinful desires, the more of a grip they gain over us. But, as with any addiction, the less we feed it, the weaker it becomes.

In the Bible James says it well, "Resist the devil, and he will flee from you. Draw near to God and He will draw near to you" (James 4:7). I love this Scripture because it's not just "DON'T DO", but right after those two words are the next two: "DRAW NEAR." You need not just avoid but you must also take in.

We would all agree that an unhealthy diet plan of simply "stopping eating" will never work as a healthy alternative. That's anorexia. But a healthy diet plan is to both "stop eating" the bad foods that are unhealthy and "start eating" the good foods for a heathy lifestyle. It's both "don't do" and "do." Starve out the unhealthy spiritual intake and indulge with a healthy intake of what is spiritually good for you.

3: CORNER IT.

Sin, like any other evil enemy, thrives amongst its allies (bitterness, un-forgiveness, discouragement, are some that come to mind). To wage effective war against sin, therefore, we must deprive it of opportunities to gain strength with it's partners.

Most sin lives and lurks in environments where they gain strength from unhealthy alliances. Lust and deception go together. Un-forgiveness and bitterness go together. Betrayal and mistrust work together. So remove the partner from it, corner it, and don't let it escape. In other words, when sin wants to find more strength from other areas of dysfunction in your life, corner it so it can't strengthen itself. Isolate it and place it under the authority of Jesus so it can never return.

This means we need to study the particular triggers of

sin in our lives. Most of the time it's a partnership of sinful emotions partnering with sinful habits. Lust is greatly weakened when it cannot appeal to fatigue, emotional need, loneliness and shame. It's more difficult to succumb to envy when you're soaking your heart in the presence of God. Sinful resentment often melts away when you are spending time with exceptionally kind, forgiving people. Basically, an effective fight against an unstoppable sin will often involve thoughtful consideration to your sleep, exercise, diet, emotional life and relationships.

4: OVERWHELM IT.

With God in our lives as Christians, we have everything we need for a satisfying life with Jesus that is free from the control of sin. In the gospel, God has given us the resources that we need to deal with unstoppable sins.

The first is patience. The gospel means that God has "perfect patience" for us even amidst our struggles with nagging sins. In the Bible, 1 Timothy 1:16 says:

> But God had mercy on me so that Christ Jesus could use me as a prime example of his great patience with even the worst sinners. Then others will realize that they, too, can believe in him and receive eternal life. To stop unstoppable sin in our lives, we need to know that God has not given up on us. Even when we have lost patience with ourselves, God is a patient Father, always calling us back to himself.

The second is grace. The Bible also says in Romans 5:20, "As people sinned more and more, God's wonderful grace became more abundant."

If you feel like you can't stop it and that this sin is too strong, God reminds us that the best way to counter the growing strength of sin in our life is to confront it with an even stronger and more potent alternative: Grace!

Grace will always overpower sin. Because God's grace is sufficient and we are not (2 Corinthians 12:9). When we don't have the strength to fight, God always does. The greatest strength that can overcome sin will always be grace, because grace comes from Jesus who went to the cross and conquered every sin you will ever face! God knows what you need so let grace conquer! This power can only come from God. The power to overcome unstoppable sins is in 2 Peter 1:3, "His divine power has given us everything we need for a godly life through our knowledge of him who called us by his own glory and goodness."

His Spirit gives us strength beyond ourselves with which to fight. His presence gives us the promise of a sustainable and lasting joy. However strong the unstoppable sins may seem, it is truly possible in Christ to "not be overcome by evil, but overcome evil with good" (Romans 12:21).

As I mentioned in Chapter Zero, I didn't grow up as a Christian. I was conditioned for 22 years to live by my own rules. My life consisted of going out Thursday through Sunday partying, drinking and engaging in unhealthy sexual relationships. What and who I surrounded myself with wasn't the best for me. So after finding Christ in college, there was a new normal for the spiritual, emotional and relational areas of my life. This new normal was wonderful, satisfying and I loved it. But while I was now a Christian, I found myself still doing some of the things I didn't want to do and the things I did want to do, I wasn't doing. So I put myself in a position to stop these unstoppable sins once and for all.

Here's how I put these different spiritual postures to work...

I started hating my sins. I made it a regular habit to imagine what my life would be like if I didn't find Jesus. I told people about what I could have been if it wasn't for Jesus saving me and making me new again. I shared my testimony on how terrible my sinful choices were, which further fueled my hate for sin and increased my love of Christ. I was so grateful that I started a habit of journaling regularly. I wrote short simple sentences of how grateful I was for salvation and how much God blessed me with a hope and a future, which helped me to hate my sin all the more.

I starved out the sin in my life by choosing to replace my thoughts with God's thoughts. I used to live by my own rules. Alan's rules seemed fun at the time but resulted in leaving me with disappointment. One of those rules was "you only live once so eat, drink and have fun." This caused me to take stupid risks of drinking with friends till I was drunk, blowing off grades for a good time, and living life for only in the "now" without thought of consequences. I followed the way of what culture told me a man was, what success was, and what life was supposed to be about (sex, money and pleasure). What I told me and what culture told me I found out were wrong. Because of Jesus, I now know who I am and how I am made, I know what it takes for me to thrive, to be satisfied and to truly enjoy life. So I starved out those thoughts and "rules" with God's thoughts and commands found in the bible. One of my life verses is found in John 10:10, "The enemy comes to steal, kill and destroy. But I have come that you may have life, life to the full."

This Scripture verse gave me permission to still enjoy life to the full but with God's grace and by God's ways. The end result of what my future was outside of God was always going to be death. Because that's what the end of living a selfish, sinful life will always get you (Romans 5:8). But Jesus is life (John 14:6) and when you choose to live like Christ, and when you make it not about you, your wants or even your dreams, and instead make it about God, His wants and His dreams for your life, you will find true life. When you delight in the Lord, He gives you the desires of your heart (Psalm 37:4). When you choose Jesus, you want to see people forgiven, the hungry fed, the broken healed, the bound set free, etc. When you starve out sin and feed on the desires that are found in the Bible, those desires that are Christ's become your desires. His convictions become your convictions. His conduct becomes your conduct.

One of my anchor verses in life which speaks to this new normal is found in Galatians 2:20:

> For you have been crucified with Christ and it's no longer you who live but Christ who lives in you and this life you now live you live for Jesus who loves you and gave Himself for you.

When you become like Christ you won't desire to sin or desire to hurt yourselves and others. Because your thoughts become His thoughts. Your ways become His ways. Your life becomes His life. It belongs to Jesus now. And that's a great thing!

I also cornered the loneliness that I felt. I was used to going out every night and partying with my friends. To change that lifestyle I resisted going out to the clubs and to parties. I just didn't trust myself and my choices so I stayed home on the weekends. That brought me to a place of resenting the weekend when everyone else was looking forward to the weekend. I started feeling lonely, depressed, second-guessing my salvation choice. I called a friend at that time and she showed me I wasn't alone, but that I not only had her but all of my friends in my church community. They showed me that there were other ways to have fun that didn't involve my old life! So I submerged myself in my church and found the best friends I could have asked for! Not only that I found my wife, Heidi, my very best friend, who was part of that community! I was looking for long-lasting relationship in the wrong places with the wrong people when I wasn't living for Christ.

Now, when I gave my life to Christ, I found the girl of my dreams and have the family I always hoped for.

I overwhelmed sin by becoming overwhelmed by God's grace. I did whatever I could to find the presence of God. I went to prayer meetings. I went to worship services. I went to Bible studies. I kept putting myself in places where the presence of God was so seen and heard, that my old sinful nature had no place to go. It's like the sinful desires that I thought were so big and powerful were slowly suffocating. Psalm 90:12-15 says it best:

> Help us to remember that our days are numbered, and help us to interpret our lives correctly. Set your wisdom deeply in our hearts...Only you can satisfy our hearts, filling us with songs of joy to the end of our days. We've been overwhelmed with grief; come now and overwhelm us with gladness.

You can be overwhelmed by many things in life: grief, stress, career, finances, depression, fear. But it's impossible to be overwhelmed by the presence of sin when we are overwhelmed by the presence of God. Unstoppable sins can be stopped. The things that once controlled my life like approval of others, alcohol, needing a girlfriend to feel loved, addictive substances, pride, sexual addiction, filthy talk, "fomo", my reputation and money no longer control me. I am free and you can be too!

CHAPTER 5 QUESTIONS

1. Is talking about sin easy or hard for you?

2. Revisit the different ways sin can affect you:

- Sin deceives you (Genesis 3:13).
- Sin desires you (Genesis 4:7).
- Sin destroys you (Genesis 6:7).
- Sin wages war over you (Romans 7:23).
- Sin entices you (James 1:14).
- Sin entangles you (Hebrews 12:1).

Which one do you identify with most?

3. How has health or lack of health effected the other parts of your life?

4. Talk about your own "spirit is willing but the flesh is weak" moments in your life.

5. Which posture are you drawn to most as you prepare to fight your own sin battles and why?

- Hate it
- Starve it
- Corner it
- Overwhelm it!

6

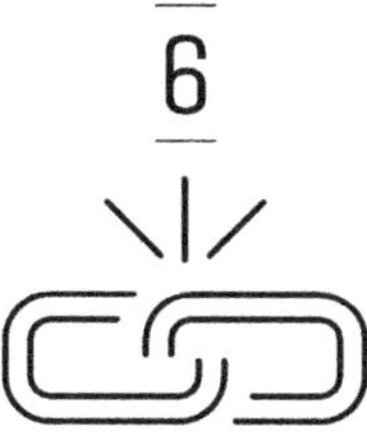

FREEING

FINDING FREEDOM FROM SEXUAL ADDICTION

If there is an issue that I hear more and more talked about with young adults, men and frankly many in the church, it is the issue of pornography. Personally, my discussions are more frequent than ever before because porn is more accessible than ever. It seems to make sense that the more accessible lust is, the more acceptable lust is. Which is why we need to create contexts for more conversations on this matter of sexual brokenness with this generation.

Sex is in the Bible. The nature of sex is to be connected and whole with another person (Genesis 2:24). In the context of marriage, being connected to your spouse is a healthy good thing, the way God intended. Sex in the confines of marriage is supposed to bond you to that other person so that you want nothing else but to be with them, to be intimate with them and to love them. That's why divorce is so hard on a couple. They are glued together and are literally being psychologically, physically and emotionally ripped apart from being bonded to each other.

Porn has the same effect. Instead of being "glued" to another person you become addicted to your screens.

You become psychologically, physically and emotionally connected to the images you look at and it bonds you to a false life in pornography; and it's just as hard to rip yourself away from it (1 Corinthians 6:16). Because of the nature of sex and how it was designed it is meant to cause you to be "addicted", in a way, with the person you are intimate with; which is why your "crazy ex" is acting the way they do, because they "just can't quit you."

Porn's addiction is powerful and when you finally find the person of your dreams, you have to "divorce" yourself from your computer images so you can bond to the girl or the guy that you are pursuing. However when you try to separate yourself from the screen, you find you can't quit because you are "addicted" or "fused" to the porn lifestyle and addiction.

It seems we've always been a sexualized culture and that's why the Bible addresses the issues of sexuality with wisdom (Proverbs 7, John 4:16-18, 1 Corinthians 6:12-20, 1 Thessalonians 4:3-4, 1 Peter 1:15). God's not outta touch… He gets it! "Pornea" is the Greek word from which we get the word "porn"; it's found in Scripture 32 times (Matthew 5:32, Romans 1:29-31, 1 Corinthians 5:1, Galatians 5:19-20, Jude 1:7, etc); so porn has been around us from the days of the Bible. But it became mainstream in 1953 with the introduction of Playboy, and from there it has become a 10 billion dollar industry (making more money than our professional sports of football, basketball and baseball combined.) You might say, "Well, I don't pay for it." And I will say, "but your click frequency creates advertising opportunities for disgusting companies to profit from them."

So every click of your mouse and log-on to their site is a dollar sign keeping the industry nice and strong to produce more.

An article came out recently in Time magazine on this issue of pornography and its affects on human beings. The article highlighted a generation of young people, saying that they have had enough of pornography and they simply don't want it anymore. These young people (not specified as Christian but simply young people, which is interesting) are saying they grew up with internet porn and are becoming advocates of turning it off. To have those who have not read the Bible and who don't seem to profess to be Christian come to the revelation that porn is damaging to their health is pretty phenomenal. The article says this:

> A growing number of young men are convinced that their sexual responses have been sabotaged because their brains were virtually marinated in porn when they were adolescents. Their generation has consumed explicit content in quantities and varieties never before possible on devices designed to deliver content swiftly and privately all at an age when their brains were more plastic—more prone to permanent change...." (Time, April 11, 2016).

The church has been sounding the alarm and now the upcoming generation is joining in. This new revelation to these young people is not catching God by surprise. God knows the power of the brain and what these images can do. That's why God was crystal clear when He said, "Do not be conformed to this world but be transformed by the renewing of your mind" (Romans 12:1-2). When it comes to your brain, these online images will do damage. What you see and look at does make an impression. Every good experience (love, joy, peace) creates a pattern in your brain, but so does every negative experience, specifically negative sexual experiences. You are highly impressionable. So fill your head with good things to become a healthy person.

One of the leading researchers in this is William Struthers. He's a Christian bio-psychologist and he wrote a book called "Wired for Intimacy." He examines what the Bible says, and what biology and current medicine have to say about how we react physically, mentally and emotionally to sex. He says:

> As we fall deeper into the mental habit of fixating on images, the exposure to them creates neural pathways. Like a path that's created in the woods with each successive hiker, so do the neural paths set the course for the next time an erotic image is viewed. Over time, these neural paths become wider, as they are repeatedly traveled with each exposure to pornography.

Basically, when you engage in pornographic behavior, you are creating a "pleasure path" that you essentially pioneer into your brain. The path you carve out in your mind is a path you don't want to continue to head down, because this path will lead you to the same places in your brain and give you the same results that heroin or cocaine do. We are essentially saying sex and drugs create the same neural pleasure paths in your brain. And once those paths are created, they are more and more easily traveled down.

I lived in Arizona and hiking is a common past time. But there are warning signs, especially on dangerous parts of the trails, that give hikers warnings NOT to venture off the trail. This sign is for those avid adventurers who like to not just follow the path in front of them but to also form new ones. These hikers don't listen and want to leave the trail to access an undiscovered part of the landscape. They choose a new direction and create a new path because of their lust for adventure. Sadly, some have met their end and you can even see memorials dedicated to hikers who decided to take it upon themselves to create these new paths, but were unaware of the dangers that were present. Their desire to form a new path wasn't safe and they fell to their death.

Your brain is an uncharted wilderness with select, beautiful trails. The paths that are there are mostly from good experiences and from memories. But porn's desire compels you to leave those trails and make a new trail. This trail is a rough cut-through at first. But because of what you feel when you go on this cut-through, you keep taking it; and then it wears through to become a path. The more we travel down this neurological pathway, the more it becomes a trail that we continue to head down, and the end result is addiction.

These paths are hard to avoid because porn always leaves you wanting more. According to fightthenewdrug.org:

> Because of it's addictive nature, in order to just feel some sense of normality, an individual usually needs an ever-increasing dosage of porn. The result is that the material that they seek out evolves. Over time, their appetite pushes them to more hardcore versions to achieve the same level of arousal. When a person is aroused by porn their brain releases dopamine that causes them to feel pleasure. And that chemical, dopamine, creates a pathway for the porn feeling to run on.

Basically, dopamine says "this feels good so let's mark this path so we remember to follow it next time." When a person is aroused by sex in marriage, it's a good thing for the dopamine to be released. But in the context of porn....it's not good.

Living during Minnesota winters, there are plenty of opportunities to create new paths. After a fresh snowfall, that white blanket of snow is just waiting for someone to make their mark. My kids and I will wrap ourselves up in our Columbia jackets, boots, and hats and head out into that flawless winter wonderland to pioneer a path across the yard. I make the first steps and who are coming up behind me? My kids are following in my steps and walking behind me in the path that I have made. Once we've gone far enough we'll turn around and we will follow that same path back again. And for days after that, that path gets used to get to the sidewalk, get to the mailbox etc.

Each step makes an imprint and forges a path that others who venture our way will soon follow.

The brain is similar to this. Think of the neurological pathways in your brain like those paths in my backyard. When you experience something, your brain makes a path. And every time you go back to that experience, the path gets more established. It's because of this biological phenomenon that you have the ability to pick up a guitar after years of practice and are able to play with little effort. It's your uncanny ability to play a game of pick-up football like "Uncle Rico" from Napoleon Dynamite and throw that pigskin a quarter mile to show them you still got it. Now consider how years of prolonged exposure to watching pornography effects your brain. As you watch pornography, you are "creating paths" in your brain to respond sexually to images on a screen. Just as playing an instrument or playing sports changes your brain, watching pornography changes your brain.

As a Christian, we have paths that we can follow, ancient paths that have been there and are available to us to follow before we ever saw pornography. These paths are ancient paths that keep you healthy in your mind and heart as they lead you back to the places where God can heal, develop and inspire you. Jeremiah 6:16 says, "This is what the LORD says: 'Stand at the crossroads and look; ask for the ancient paths, ask where the good way is, and walk in it, and you will find rest for your souls.'"

We are all in need of rest for our souls. It starts by leaving the familiar porn paths and returning to the trails that matter to you that are connected to faith, family and friends...not the glow of your screen. It's easy to follow your most recent paths to pleasure. It's a lot harder to uncover those ancient paths back to God again. Following God is like finding that perfect path in the woods. You walk that path regularly as you come back to that path again and again. That path is forged by prayer, worship, Scripture, community, etc. You keep going back because it's beautiful and it's peaceful. Each venture back over that path you discover new expressions of God's truth you didn't realize before. But we all have experienced seasons when we frequent those paths less and less because of life change, busyness, distractions, relationship influence, etc. That path that was once easy to find has now become overgrown. But the reality is that it's still there. Because God is still there. That "ancient path" back to Him is always there, ready and waiting for you to find Him again.

I've chosen to engage this topic with the young people I've been pastoring because I really believe you can be free from porn and sexual immorality and stay free. However, I've experienced an anticipated response from culture, specifically from young guys, where it seems they believe failure in this area is normal and lust is to be expected. A group of guys sitting around affirming their expected failures involving their sex drive is not God's best for these guys, or for you! While being vulnerable about our sexual failures can be viewed as progress, it's not the desired end result for any young person battling porn addiction to remain just talking about it and never breaking its hold on their life. Sexual dysfunction (porn, masturbation, casual sex, friends with benefits, etc.) can become accepted and tolerated by others. Even believers in a spiritual community can become comfortable with it (you can read about this in 1 and 2 Corinthians in the city of Corinth). But we can and should live free from the effects of pornography in our culture.

For me personally, porn is only a "click" away and I am choosing every day to live free and clear from its addictive tendencies. I really want to be an example of a follower of Christ who can live free, rather than giving the excuses I've heard: "well as guys we aren't really ever 'free' from lust, you know?"...this is not and does not have to be true. I refuse to be the pastor that has "the gap" of what happens publicly and what happens privately. I want my public and private life accountable. That's how pastors, leaders, husbands, fathers, sons, implode because there is a slow erosion of character in the gaps between how people see us on our "platforms" at work, at school, at home with our families etc and who we are when no one is looking. I will do whatever it takes to not have "the gap" and live a life that who I am on-stage is who I am off-stage. It's a fight, and I am choosing Jesus. And when I choose Jesus that always means that I am winning.

I still have contact with young people who are part of the #fightclub. To some degree we are all "young Brad Pitts" fighting ourselves and overcoming our own personal battles of sexual addiction...all the while believing "you do not talk about fight club". We all know it's there. So let's be a generation of believers who have chosen to fight and win! I have talked to guys who have started with the struggle but who are now free from porn because they chose to be honest, accountable, hungry for God, loving their wives, giving their all, honoring all the women around them, loving God and pursuing Jesus with everything they've got. It's not being a weird Christian who has decided to move to a cave without electricity, writing on a coal shovel like Abe Lincoln instead of an iPad, and using the telegraph to avoid the dangers of sex in the media. It is about resisting. Sure! But it's also about "drawing near." I think in the Christian culture we have a heavy emphasis on "not sinning" but we also need an equal if not more emphasis on pursuing Jesus!

The Bible says, "Submit to God. Resist the devil. Draw near to God and He will draw near to you" (James 4:7). I know the devil isn't behind every pornographic temptation. But the idea there is RESIST. We know how to put filters on our phones, software on our computers, develop community groups to share our struggles. So we choose to resist and we can be good at it. But are we as good at drawing near or in other words, pursuing God? If not, we need to be. Because it's not just about resisting and stopping bad behaviors but it's also about starting new ones. Some of these new behaviors involve praying, reading your Bible, worshiping and repentance.

The Greek word for "repent" in the New Testament is "metanoeo" which means "to change one's mind." That's what we've been talking about. Literally, changing the way you think. This is why living a life of regular repentance is so key to The New Young Christian. Repenting is turning from sin with contrition and moving towards God and pursuing Him.

Repentance is similar to heading for a drive down the freeway but you realize you are going the wrong way. Not only that but there is traffic coming straight at you! You need to turn around and go the other way. Repentance is realizing you are heading dangerously in the wrong direction so you turn around. And not just turn around but you also do one important thing: you move forward. As Christians, we can be great at turning from sin but bad at moving forward. Repentance without progression is spiritually "moving in circles." Driving in circles on a freeway is just as deadly as going the wrong way! That's why the strength of repentance is not only in changing directions by saying "forgive me", but it's also moving forward in obedience. Maybe our battle with porn is less of a spiritual roller-coaster and more of a "spiritual tilt-a-whirl." If you've seen this ride at an amusement park, it's less about going up and down and more about making you dizzy while moving in circles. This "spiritual ride" is brutal on the Christians because it doesn't move you forward, but keeps you in an endless circle of "I'm sorry God, I didn't mean to" then to "God forgives me" to "God loves me" to "I'm sorry God, I didn't mean to" back to "God forgives me," etc.

This is why so many incredible young people give up or say to me overcoming porn is "too difficult." It feels like there is no progress. That you are trapped in the same spiritual spot for days, weeks, months and even years! That's why freedom from sexual addiction is less about trying to give you 1001 ways to stop looking at porn and more about giving you a singular goal: "pursue Jesus."

Moving forward and following Him without stopping.

The best way to overcome temptation is to follow the One who overcame temptation and didn't sin. That's Jesus. So seek Christ. Worship. Pray. Fill your room with the praises of Christ. Seek the cross. Love God with all your heart, soul, mind and strength. I guarantee it is a lot harder to look at pornography when you've got worship music playing in your room, with your Bible on your bed and a Scripture graphic on your phone that you are trying to commit to memory. You are much less likely to turn to porn when God means so much to you. Porn will lose its pull over you when God matters more to you. What we are saying is...

The struggle is real but so is Jesus.

Make Jesus your pursuit. If lust says "I want it" then let pursuit say "I want God." If pride says, "I got this on my own" then let pursuit say "I got God and He's with me." If weakness says "I can't do it, I wanna give up" then let pursuit say "God can do it: keep going. " His strength is made perfect in my weakness (2 Corinthians 12:9). Overcoming porn starts with Jesus and letting Him into your life. Not religion or performance-based faith where we try and try yet keep messing up, but a true encounter with Christ. Your authentic encounter with Jesus is the fuel to keep going, keep seeking and keeping watch for what God will do.

Your personal relationship with Jesus is never a 'one-and-done' but it's a daily pursuit with Christ. Many of us live our Christian lives as a decision to follow Jesus but to live a life of discipleship requires a determination well beyond your decision. That's why discipleship celebrates progress more than success. Winning the war on porn in your life is not striving for overnight success but is focusing on a long obedience in God's direction. Just like any addiction, porn is one day at a time. Pursuit with Jesus is one day at a time as well. You are on a long journey to know Him more and to let Him change you from the inside out one day at a time.

This is where living intentionally must become a natural part of your life. I have to be intentional with what I see, what I do, how I live, how I love, how I father, how I worship, how I seek God. Cold turkey quitting doesn't seem to work for most people. It can be discouraging, overwhelming and defeating. That's why you need a plan of attack.

Here is a 9-Point Plan to continue to walk in freedom from pornography.

1: LIVE DAILY IN FREEDOM.

The reality is you are built to talk to God. When you ask God to forgive you, He does! The Bible says in 1 John 1:9 "If we confess our sins, he is faithful and just and will forgive us our sins and purify us from all unrighteousness." When you ask God to forgive you, it puts you back in alignment to God's holiness and godliness. That's God's gift to you. That's mercy which is new every day for you.

God says this about you:

"The faithful love of the Lord never ends! His mercies never cease. Great is his faithfulness; His mercies begin afresh each morning" (Lamentations 3:22-23).

I've often defined grace and mercy this way: Mercy is forgiveness you don't deserve and grace is the blessing of God and His affirmation of you that you didn't earn. And it's all because of Jesus. So, when you choose to pray every day (regardless of what happened yesterday), you stay close to God and you are reminded of who you are and what Jesus has done for you.

2: STOP LETTING TEMPTATIONS DISQUALIFY YOU.

There is a big difference between temptation and sin. Even Jesus was tempted in all things as we are yet did not sin (Hebrews 4:15). Experiencing temptations doesn't make you evil, if anything, it makes you like Jesus. The temptations that we experience are not sins. The difference between Jesus and you is that Jesus didn't agree with the sin He was tempted with. When we agree with the desire (embracing sin and acting on it) instead of resisting it, that's what makes us sin. You are not disqualified from being a Christian because of your temptations, but because of your sinful actions. The distinction between temptation and sin is hard at times to differentiate between. Especially in the context of sexual desires.

Here's what I mean...

Sex is enticing to you because God put the desire in you to be fruitful as a human being (Genesis 1:28). So, to desire sex isn't wrong. If you are tempted to have sex, the temptation isn't wrong either. But to give in to the temptation (outside of marriage) is. When you start to think what sex would be like with that person, that would be the beginning of sin. It's sin because you stopped resisting and started to let your mind go rather than restraining yourself and taking your thoughts captive. It seems hard to believe in our current day, but sexual fantasy about someone, while it is only in the mind and is harmless to them, is harmful to you and is hurtful to God.

Sin in the Greek original context is "parakoe" which literally means "to refuse to hear and follow God's command." A great example of this particular word is found when God is encouraging us to take every disobedient thought captive and make it obedient to Christ (2 Corinthians 10:5-6). When we let our minds run wild and fantasize, that is considered sin according to the Bible (Matthew 5:27-28). So before it becomes sin, stop temptation in its tracks. Take it captive and give it to Jesus in repentance. Obsess about Jesus instead of obsessing about the opposite sex. Stop beating yourself up over temptation and get serious instead about resisting sin and passionately pursuing Jesus.

3: RECOGNIZE SHAME IN YOUR LIFE.

There is a difference between feeling bad and being bad. We love Oreo's at my house. When my son sneaks an

Oreo before dinner when he knows he can't have one, he feels bad. That's called guilt…he knows he's guilty and if I find out, he's doing 20 sit-ups for that "sweet violation." Even though he feels guilty, he's still my son. I even remind him that he is still my "strong, brave, lover of Jesus" (that's what his name - Magnus Anders Kristian - means). He feels bad because he made a bad choice. But he still is and will always be my son. That's the difference between shame and conviction. Conviction from God says, "I did a bad thing." Shame is different. Shame says, "I am a bad person." It attacks your identity. Shame tries to tell my boy "you're a bad son." Conviction tells my boy, "you made a bad choice…but you're still a good son." Once you recognize the effects of shame in your life, you won't be ruled by it.

4: ACCEPT YOUR IDENTITY FROM GOD NOT YOUR SIN.

Your temptation doesn't define you. As a Christian, if you are tempted to want to have sex, that doesn't make you a porn addict (see previous point). Your temptation isn't your identity. I have talked to guys who have said to me, "Alan, I'm a porn addict." When I ask them about it, they say it is because they looked at porn or have had lustful thoughts on a regular basis. I always ask if they have asked God to forgive them and they usually say yes. Then I say, "Man, if you know Christ, you are a 'son' of God…not a porn addict" (Romans 8:15). Your temptations or even past sins do not define you if you are follower of Christ. You are a Christian. As a Christian, you will struggle with sin. That's normal. You are not a sinner in need of salvation (that's who you were!) But you are a saved son of God. The Bible confirms this:

> Do not be deceived: neither the sexually immoral nor idolaters nor adulterers nor men who have sex with men nor thieves nor the greedy nor drunkards nor slanderers nor swindlers will inherit the kingdom of God. And that is what some of you were. But you were washed, you were sanctified, you were justified in the name of the Lord Jesus Christ and by the Spirit of God (1 Corinthians 6:9-11).

That is what you were. Maybe you can identify with some of these struggles. As a Christian, you are now a child of God! You are a lover of Jesus! You are forgiven! You are no longer a sinner in need salvation but you are a Christian in need of forgiveness! Your temptation and your sin doesn't define you…God does. Your bad behaviors are not your identity. Many of us choose to live from and act out our "sin alias." As a Christian, your sin alias is when your bad decisions define you and tell you who you are, and you unfortunately start living more and more from this fake identity, spending more and more of your time proving who you're not. But when you get in the presence of Jesus, your alias is exposed. The true you is seen and heard. Those bad choices you made are under the blood of Christ. You are not your choices but you are forgiven by Jesus and you live from your true identity again as a "child of God." If Jesus needed reminding that He was the

Son of God before He went into the desert to experience temptation, so do you (Matthew 3:17).

5: AVOID ISOLATION.

God put others in our lives to encourage us, so that we can share with each other, be vulnerable and to find hope in times of struggle. In other words, God put people in your life so that you can "give an account." In the church, we call this "accountability." God desires for us to have others in our life to hold us accountable. While this word is loved by some and not by others, think of this word in the practical sense of accounting. Accountability is simply "giving an account" of what your life is adding up to. Certain decisions you make will "add" to your life and other choices you make will "subtract" from your life. Following Jesus and living a life in obedience to Him will always "add" to what God is doing in you. But resisting Jesus and living in disobedience will always "take away" from what God has originally intended for you. You may not feel it in the moment but over time, those decisions will add up.

Being accountable to someone is as simple as telling them if you are "in the red" or if you are "in the black." Just like an accountant who is managing financials, being "in the red" means you are functioning with a shortage of funds. But if you are "in the black" that means you are functioning with an adequate or an abundance of income. Whether you are in the black or the red, God is using others to inspire you and encourage you to help you overcome. I have friends I can call at a moment's notice to tell

I'm struggling. I am healthy today because of them in my life and have the trust to be accountable to them. I share with them my own struggles and confess to them my own personal issues I'm dealing with. Even Scripture speaks about "confessing your sins so you can be healed" (James 5:16). We know only Christ can forgive sins, but telling another person helps us to not only "speak it out loud," but it also helps us process with them so they can affirm God's forgiveness of sins in our lives, and God can speak through them to give us the wisdom to get through it.

It's easy to keep things hidden. Keeping others "in the dark" on things we are facing isn't hard. Do you want to know how to remain enslaved to a particular sin? Just keep hiding it. Tell no one about it. Keep it in the dark. Sin grows in the dark. Like that chili you said you were going to eat tomorrow but that you forgot about a few weeks ago which is now growing that "grey fur" all over the top of it. Sin grows, festers, and becomes a fungus on your spiritual life. The more you keep it covered up, hidden and out of reach from others, the more it will become rancid in your life. Consider these couple Biblical passages and meditate on them about concealing and hiding sins:

> When I kept silent, my bones wasted away through my groaning all day long. For day and night your hand was heavy on me; my strength was sapped as in the heat of summer. Then I acknowledged my sin to you and did not cover up my iniquity. I said, "I will confess my transgressions to the Lord." And you forgave the guilt of my sin (Psalm 23:3-5).

> Whoever conceals his transgressions will not prosper, but he who confesses and forsakes them will obtain mercy (Proverbs 28:13).

6: BE VULNERABLE.

One of our deepest desires and valued needs as human beings is to be known and seen. We long to have someone look at us, know every nook and cranny of our hearts, and at the end of the day still love every part of us. This is the way we were designed by God; for intimacy. I've heard it said that "intimacy" is "into me you see." Because that's just what it is—an uncovered heart, free from fear and fully seen. I want to encourage you to be vulnerable with someone.

Vulnerability isn't weak to others but wonderful to others. I repeat, vulnerability doesn't mean that you're weak, it means that you're brave enough to embrace the reality that you don't have it all together but trust God who holds it all together. Authenticity reveals "this is who I am." Vulnerability exposes "this is who I'm not." Your vulnerability shapes your originality.

I'm great at putting on a good exterior. But I'm bad at letting others look "under the hood" and see the dysfunction underneath. But as I get older, I realize that being vulnerable with people is one of the most "freeing joys" that I have experienced with another person. That's why trying to adjust yourself according to who and what others want you to be is the exact opposite of freedom and it's the least joyful. When we try to be someone else to everyone else it's simply wrong. Because when we hide the "undesirable" parts of our lives, we are building our lives on a façade rather than a foundation. Like a movie set, facades are shaky, flimsy and have an appearance but are just plywood and plastic. Foundations are the real thing and when Christ is your foundation, then you have all the permission in the world to be yourself. We are all deserving of love exactly as we are because Christ loves us and accepts us as we are (Romans 8:38-39).

7: LIVE IN GRACE.

The rhythms of grace make living in freedom not in anyway like "work", but as simple as breathing. Grace permeates every area of your life as a Christian. This beautiful expression of grace (God being for you and with you) is possible only because of Jesus. The sin of pornography in your life is taken away because of Christ's work of becoming your sin, so you don't have to carry it and let it dominate it you anymore (2 Corinthians 5:21). Shame has a way of trying to keep sin around, and have you keep repenting of the same sin you already repented of last month (and the month before). But grace says you are forgiven and free from sin, because Jesus says it's the truth (John 8:36).

8: STOP ASKING GOD "TO TAKE AWAY" WHAT YOU WERE ALWAYS "MEANT TO HAVE."

Young people seem to pray "take this longing away." But God will not take the feelings of desiring sex from you because it is and has always been God's plan for you to be a sexual human being. Even if God has called you to be single (I admire that call and am amazed at the grace that God gives for those who are walking in singleness), single people are still sexual beings with sexual desires. It seems those desires aren't completely eradicated when you're called to be celibate for a season or single for life. We are all sexual beings with sexual desires. God gave us all perimeters in Scripture for us to fulfill our sexual needs. Following Scripture with our relationships and having God be a part of our sexual relationships will always be the most fulfilling despite who we are and who we are supposed to be with. But acting outside of the perimeters set by Scripture will bring hurt and difficulty. Culture has disorientated and confused this generation to think that porn is normal. Not just sites that are raunchy, but "rated M for mature" on our TV shows seems to prove to us that "what's happening under the sheets" is OK. But let's be honest, it's soft-core porn and we have to learn how to navigate that as Christians. Managing your sexual desires isn't going to be found in "God take it away" as a solution. But instead, the answer will be found with a "God make a way" solution instead. God make a way for me to read more Scriptures, make a way to worship longer, make a way for me to pray longer, etc. As we've been mentioning, all of these desires that God is making a way for, will always come through with more encounters with Jesus in worship, the Bible, in community, etc.

9: THINK LONG-TERM.

We want to live in the moment. We are conditioned to live in the moment. But God always speaks of seasons, seed, growth and harvest. We are meant to go for the long haul of life and it's not easy. Pornography allows for an easy way out. It's the pleasure of a sexual relationship without the commitment or hard work of a real relationship. I've been married for over 22 years and the truth is marriage takes effort. It's the long obedience with God that matters in the end. We have been told that overnight success is normal and in turn, overnight relationships and it's benefits are normal. Porn says you can have the benefits of sex without the cost of a relationship. Our culture celebrates the benefits without the hard work.

The lie is that porn actually costs you so much more and the end result is always loss, hurt, pain and selfishness.

Overcoming the painful effects of lust in your life will take time but it can be done. Don't cut short the legacy God always had in mind for you and your family for a brief moment of pleasure. It's just not worth it.

CHAPTER 6 QUESTIONS

1. Does it shock you that non-Christian young adults are desiring to resist pornography? Have Christians taken a lighter approach to pornography? Why?

2. How early were you when you were exposed to pornography? How did it affect you? How does it affect the opposite-sex relationships around you?

3. James 4:7 says, "Submit to God. Resist the devil. Draw near to God and He will draw near to you." How does this Scripture help you in defending yourself against pornography?

4. Culture seems to give us the impression that the repercussions of sex outside of marriage are not a big deal. Do you agree?

5. Have you allowed your temptations to disqualify you? How?

6. Do you agree with the idea that shame attacks your identity and conviction affirms your choices?

7

SHARING

BELIEVING IN JESUS AND EXPRESSING YOUR FAITH NATURALLY

"When I think of Easter, it means we have bunnies, chocolates, tulips and egg hunts." Wait, no empty tomb in that list? Yes, there was no reference to Christ, because the person I am quoting is a young man from Europe. When I was in Belgium I was conducting an interview on the street, asking people what Easter meant to them simply as a way to engage in conversation on spiritual matters with the locals and document their story. It was during this that I met the young guy quoted above, who had no reference to Christianity or faith when it comes to the holiday of Easter. It was in that moment of capturing his story and spending time with him that I eventually had the chance to share about who Jesus was and why I believed what I believed. He didn't become a Christian that day, but he heard for the first time that Easter is more than just candy and bunnies. He heard that Jesus died on a cross and actually resurrected from the dead to show the world that death is conquered and that eternal life is for everyone. I shared with him about Jesus' life, death and His resurrection. I believe that the resurrection is the most significant reason that what we believe, who we pray to, and what we are living for is real. The Bible says it this way:

> The message we preach is Christ, who has been raised from the dead. So how could any of you possibly say there is no resurrection of the dead? For if there is no such thing as a resurrection from the dead, then not even Christ has been raised. And if Christ has not been raised, all of our preaching has been for nothing and your faith is useless. (1 Corinthians 15:10–14)

So this begs the question, can we have confidence in the truth of this event that took place over 2,000 years ago? The answer is yes, and we truly need to be confident of this truth as we look to share our faith with men like the one I encountered in Belgium.

To help you feel confident, here's 4 facts as to why the resurrection is the best account of who Jesus truly is:

FACT 1: WE KNOW JESUS DIED ON THE CROSS.

There is no scholarly debate about this. Why? Because a number of different writers in the Bible make the claim throughout the Scriptures. We have extra-biblical Christian writers like Ignatius and Clement of Rome who spoke about Christ's death. We also have non-Christian writers like Tacitus and Josephus at the end of the first century who claim Jesus came and died on the cross. Like the CNN of their day, they talked about it and recorded it in their history books. Tacitus writes this about Christ's crucifixion and what happened:

> Consequently, to get rid of the report, Nero fastened the guilt and inflicted the most exquisite tortures on a class hated for their abominations, called Christians by the populace. Christus, from whom the name had its origin, suffered the extreme penalty during the reign of Tiberius at the hands of one of our procurators, Pontius Pilatus.

Not to mention, Christians wouldn't make up the fact the Messiah was crucified. The cross was a symbol of shame, disdain and rejection in the modern Jewish/ Roman world. So to glorify such an event wouldn't have helped in their "Jesus Will Make Your Life Awesome" PR campaign. The resurrection wasn't a fabricated event to bolster followers. It was real.

FACT 2: THE TOMB WAS EMPTY.

First, the tomb was discovered by women. During first century Palestine, a women's testimony was considered worthless. Unfortunately, women weren't educated like men back in the first century. So this begs the question why women would have discovered the empty tomb. This helps the credibility or the probability that it was a valid event. Putting a woman at the forefront of this story shows to the world that the uniqueness of the claim of resurrection is as unique as women being the first, official herald's of this amazing discovery! Jesus and Christianity support a woman's voice and testimony in making this discovery of the empty tomb. According to Josephus, the testimony of women was regarded as so worthless that it could not even be admitted into a Jewish court of law (thank God for the strides we've made in recognizing and celebrating women!). And yet, Jesus chose to rely on their testimony as the first to witness His event. A legendary story to go around the world would have certainly placed men discovering the tomb. But Jesus revealed it and gave it to the oppressed to share. Not the best move if you were trying to spread "fake news" about a "fake resurrection." All the more reason to believe Jesus was who He said He was.

Also, we read that the religious leaders tried to claim that the disciples stole the body. Why make that up? Because the body was gone and the tomb was empty. There was no logical explanation for where the body went. Jesus' grave back then wasn't a hole in the ground but a cave with a massive stone in front of it, and it was guarded by soldiers day and night. Before the famous "three days and He rose" moment, the religious community had an idea that the disciples might try to fake Jesus' resurrection. So they made sure that this wouldn't happen.

See what one of the eye witnesses, and one of Jesus' disciples Matthew says:

> The next day, the day after Preparation Day for Passover, the chief priests and the Pharisees went together to Pilate. They said to him, "Our master, we remember that this impostor claimed that he would rise from the dead after three days. So please, order the tomb to be sealed until after the third day. Seal it so that his disciples can't come and steal the corpse and tell people he rose from the dead. Then the last deception would be worse than the first!"
>
> "I will send soldiers to guard the tomb," Pilate replied. "Go with them and make the tomb as secure as possible." So they left and sealed the stone, and Pilate's soldiers secured the tomb (Matthew 27:62-66).

It wasn't fake. The tomb was empty, proving to the world that Jesus is who He says He is.

FACT 3: JESUS APPEARED TO PEOPLE.

Jesus appeared to Saul who was persecuting Christians. That moment was so significant to him that he left his role as lead persecutor of Christians and became a lead proclaimer of Jesus. Jesus appeared to over 500 people and many others. See the reference below from Paul's testimony in his letter to Christians in Corinth who were also doubting if the resurrection was real:

> He was buried in a tomb and was raised from the dead after three days, as foretold in the Scriptures. Then he appeared to Peter the Rock and to the 12 apostles. He also appeared to more than 500 of his followers at the same time, most of whom are still alive as I write this, though a few have passed away. Then he appeared to James and to all the apostles. Last of all he appeared in front of me (1 Corinthians 15:4–8).

We have good evidence from the gospels that neither James nor any of Jesus' younger brothers believed in him during his lifetime. There is no reason to think that the early church would generate fictitious stories concerning the unbelief of Jesus' family had they been faithful followers all along. But it is indisputable that James and his brothers did become active Christian believers following Jesus' death. We all know that those closest to us are the hardest to convince when you have a dream, an idea or a claim that you are making about yourself and your future, often because your family wants what's best for you and wants to see you succeed. Anything that would jeopardize that or cause harm, they would fight against. Declaring yourself Savior of the world is one claim that would need some convincing. And Jesus' family were eventually convinced!

FACT 4: THE DISCIPLES WERE WILLING TO DIE.

The disciples and many Christians faced horrible deaths because of their beliefs. Some were crucified like Christ, some were left to die on an island by themselves, some were lit on fire, some were fed to lions, some were covered in tar. We know you can believe a lie and essentially be "sincerely wrong" about someone. That's why Jesus' brother, James, is intriguing. Even his own brother didn't believe, but ultimately was convinced and died for his belief.

It's been shown historically that James was leader of the apostles in Jerusalem. James remained the leader of the Jerusalem church until his death around A.D. 62. This is the account of his martyrdom according to Hegesippus (a 2nd century Christian about whom little is known) which is quoted in Eusebius' Ecclesiastical History, Vol. II, ch. 23 (A.D. 323):

> James was led to the top of the temple by the Pharisees to let the people see exactly what happens to those who dare to believe in Jesus. They climbed the temple as the people shouted, reached the top and threw James from the pinnacle of the temple. It didn't kill him. He rose to his knees and began to pray for them. The Pharisees on the ground began to stone him as he prayed, while those from the roof rushed down to join the execution. All because James believed a con-man, a lie? No. Even though they were threatened with death they still believed.

For these reasons and many more, you have a good case to share with others that Jesus really did die and rise again.

So the resurrection is a certain fact and a key point as we interact with people far from Him. However, what else can we point to as evidence of the existence of God?

I was talking recently to someone who is having honest conversations and introspection about their faith. I always have believed that the more honest and sincere you can be with yourself about God, the more honest and sincere God will be with you about yourself. Whether you are embracing extreme trust in God or extreme doubt, it doesn't change God's love for you. While I was talking to this person, one of the questions asked was, "What about those who were not raised in a Christian home?"

If you grew up in a privileged home in a faith community where Jesus is declared as the Son of God, did you get a better hand dealt than the Muslim believer who believed Jesus was only a prophet and is still subject to Allah for example? As I reflected on this question, I came to understand we can reconcile this with two words.

Two words that will further help us as we interact within a culture walking away from God.

WORD 1: CREATION.

No matter where you are living, you are surrounded by creation. I have had the privilege of living in the four corners of the country. From the blue waters on the Gulf Coast, to the deserts of Phoenix, to the mountains and trees of the east coast near Washington, D.C., to the bold north of Minnesota, each offers its own beauty in creation where God can "show off." Each of these areas offers expressions of creation where God can reveal Himself in the surroundings. In the Bible, the book of Romans speaks about this truth:

> For ever since the world was created, people have seen the earth and sky. Through everything God made, they can clearly see his invisible qualities—his eternal power and divine nature. So they have no excuse for not knowing God (Romans 1:20).

Did you grasp that? God reveals "His eternal power and divine nature" so clearly that everyone is left "without excuse." The creation speaks out loudly that there is a Creator. No matter what part of the nation or the world you live in, creation reveals there is a Creator. Don't let anyone tell you that God has hidden Himself from the world. Every intelligent being lives every waking moment under the constant reminder that God is here, He is over it all, and He is powerful. People can be stubborn in their unbelief, which causes humanity to miss God's constant and persistent message. Here's a few more Scriptures to help you see God in creation:

> Faith empowers us to see that the universe was created and beautifully coordinated by the power of God's words! He spoke and the invisible realm gave birth to all that is seen (Hebrews 11:3).

For through the Son everything was created, both in the heavenly realm and on the earth, all that is seen and all that is unseen. Every seat of power, realm of government, principality, and authority—it was all created through him and for his purpose! He existed before anything was made, and now everything finds completion in him (Colossians 1:16-17).

Job, the righteous man who trusted God in suffering, wrote: "But ask the animals, and they will teach you, or the birds in the sky, and they will tell you; or speak to the earth, and it will teach you, or let the fish in the sea inform you. Which of all these does not know that the hand of the Lord has done this? In his hand is the life of every creature and the breath of all mankind (Job 12:7-10).

O Lord, our Lord, your majestic name fills the earth! Your glory is higher than the heavens… When I look at the night sky and see the work of your fingers — the moon and the stars you set in place — what are mere mortals that you should think about them, human beings that you should care for them? (Psalm 8:1, 3-4).

The heavens declare the glory of God; the skies proclaim the work of his hands. Day after day they pour forth speech; night after night they reveal knowledge. They have no speech, they use no words; no sound is heard from them. Yet their voice goes out into all the earth, their words to the ends of the world. In the

> heavens God has pitched a tent for the sun. It is like a bridegroom coming out of his chamber, like a champion rejoicing to run his course. It rises at one end of the heavens and makes its circuit to the other; nothing is deprived of its warmth (Psalm 19:1-6).

WORD 2: CONSCIOUSNESS.

There is an obviousness about God revealed to our consciousness. It says in Romans, "In reality, the truth of God is known instinctively, for God has embedded this knowledge inside every human heart" (Romans 1:19).

Scripture makes it clear that God has made the truth about Him instinctive to us by putting it in our heart, or in other words, our consciousness. Paul continues to express this truth by confirming that people without the "biblical law" still have a moral law written on their hearts:

> Even Gentiles [people who are outsiders of faith] who do not have God's written law, show that they know his law when they instinctively obey it, even without having heard it. They demonstrate that God's law is written in their hearts, for their own conscience and thoughts either accuse them or tell them they are doing right (Romans 2:14-15).

In other words, God gives us an inherent morality that we can't ignore that speaks to us about right and wrong. Without experiencing a Christian childhood or without even meeting a Christian, there is an instinctive understanding that the morality we have inside us has to come from somewhere. We can choose to ignore it or pretend it doesn't exist, but it doesn't excuse us from the reality that God is showing Himself to us in those moments.

Everyone who has ever lived has evidence then that there is a God. These major revelations will carry and confirm God's existence, and God can use these revelations to bring those far away from God into a relationship with Him. The question to those around us then is not "how will God answer those who have not heard?", but instead "what will you do with the truth you have heard?" Perhaps you are sitting there reading these words and thinking "but I am not confident enough to share my faith with others?" Well, at The New Young Christian, we have a ministry called RŌG (rogue) Saints. A RŌG Saint is someone who runs head-first into Christian skepticism. RŌG Saints choose to engage culture enthusiastically to challenge the "cultural norms." We believe that there are three essentials when engaging others to share your faith: reason, respect and relationship. We believe all three are "must-have's" when you are talking to someone who believes different than you. Each one supports the other with the balance of talking AND listening. Without love we are nothing so we choose to show the authenticity of Jesus by winning hearts not arguments. We are theological renegades who believe the most powerful apologetic is you. The Bible says it this way, "Always be prepared to give an answer to everyone who asks you to give the reason for the hope that you have." (1 Peter 3:15)

This mandate is for all of us! Whether you are confident or otherwise. So, let your faith run wild and "GO RŌG." If you want to see more articles and inspiration to help as you share your faith and to do so with confidence, please go to **roguesaint.org** ...and keep reading!

The reality that cannot be ignored by any of us is that people have questions. They are wondering if faith makes sense to them. They are wondering if God does exist. Christians need to be ready to help answer the questions that people and even culture are asking, not simply give answers to questions that people and culture aren't asking. You have to learn to read the "cultural room."

Recently, I walked into a conversation that others were having and I was throwing in my thoughts and contributing without getting the whole picture or understanding. After I asserted myself and shared my "super amazing insight", I suddenly realized they weren't talking about someone's actual circumstances but they were talking about a film they had recently watched. I was hearing questions asked and giving answers to questions that aren't being asked ... and that didn't need my advice!

Read the room, Alan.

Culture is having spiritual conversations that Christians aren't invited into because we are giving answers to questions that aren't being asked. We need to stop and listen to questions and concerns of those in our community, in our workplace, in our schools. An active listener is not just hearing words but listening to questions, and they are not just giving insight to things that aren't necessary. On this journey of expressing our faith naturally we must talk to real people about real things going on and share our lives with authenticity.

For example, there is a question that many Christians seem to believe that culture is asking—so they ask it for them. It sounds like this...

> "If you were to die today, do you know where you would go?"
>
> In return, the answer given by some who are not Christians, "I would be reincarnated and come back as a part of nature based on my good works that I contribute on earth as a human being ."
>
> Then the response by Christians, "Oh. Ummm, ok. I, uh … Jesus says, ummm …"

What is the right response to the questions outsiders of faith are asking? Barna has just released the findings of a new study commissioned by the discipleship organization called Alpha USA (https://www.barna.com/research/millennials-oppose-evangelism/). The goal of the research was to better understand what Christian millennials believe about the gospel and sharing their faith. One of the revelations in particular is shocking. Though the vast majority of millennials agree with statements like "The best thing that could ever happen to someone is for them to know Jesus," things changed when asked about sharing their faith. From the report: "Almost half of millennials (47 percent) agree at least somewhat that it is wrong to share one's personal beliefs with someone of a different faith in hopes that they will one day share the same faith."

That is far higher than Gen X, Boomers and other older generations. (Gen Z wasn't included in the study.) That makes millennials the most evangelism-reluctant generation to date. In a statement included in the research, Barna Group president David Kinnaman said:

> Even after they are committed to sustaining resilient faith, we must persuade younger Christians that evangelism is an essential practice of following Jesus. The data show enormous ambivalence among millennials, in particular, about the calling to share their faith with others.

Cultivating deep, steady, resilient Christian conviction is difficult. Evangelism isn't just about saving those who need saving, but reminding ourselves that the kingdom matters, that the Bible is trustworthy, and that Jesus changes everything. The Bible puts it like this:

> Live wisely among those who are not believers, and make the most of every opportunity. Let your conversation be gracious and attractive so that you will have the right response for everyone (Colossians 4:5–6).

Have the right response. Maybe we are responding wrong- and asking the wrong questions in the first place.

Here are some issues that we are hearing about in culture right now:

- When does life start for a human being?
- How does race affect our relationships with each other?
- Can we be politically opposite but be united as humans?
- Can the gay community and the Christian community coexist?
- Resistance to authority or submission to authority?

Culture is talking about abortion, racism, injustice and bringing restoration to a world that needs it more than ever before. What are we sharing about in our churches, our communities and our homes that helps others draw nearer to Christ in light of these conversations, not in spite of them? Let's be honest, many of us shy away from hard conversation because we are afraid of 'forcing our opinions on others'. But Jesus doesn't come across in Scripture like "He is forcing His convictions upon us." Jesus preached some of the hardest messages, yet crowds continued to flock to him. Part of the reason I think that faith isn't potent in our culture is because we get nervous when the term evangelism gets brought up.

So what is evangelism really?

Let me tell you what evangelism is not:

- Having an acute knowledge of theology
- Being super bold about faith issues
- Reserved for only certain Christians
- Bringing people to church
- Being extremely educated and extraordinary

Maybe we need to see evangelism differently. Maybe evangelism was always meant to be unschooled and ordinary. Look in the book of Acts when Peter and John were sharing their faith with government officials:

> Now as they observed the confidence of Peter and John and understood that they were uneducated and untrained men, they were amazed, and began to recognize them as having been with Jesus (Acts 4:13).

Following the healing of the lame man in Acts 3, Peter and John were called before the Sanhedrin to give an account of what they were teaching the people. Peter, though only a fisherman, was filled with the Holy Spirit, and went straight to the cross and to the gospel, speaking boldly and confidently. This left the religious authorities confused. How was it that ordinary, uneducated, common men could know so much and do so many great things. How could they speak with such authority? The Sanhedrin marveled because Peter and John were 'unschooled'. This does not mean that they were ignorant or illiterate – it simply meant that they did not have recognized qualifications from the 'right' rabbinical schools. In reality, Peter and John had spent about 3 years learning directly from Jesus Himself, the Son of God, the Author of the Scriptures – they were certainly not uneducated in the things of God. They were close to Jesus.

The Sanhedrin "took note that these men had been with Jesus". Being with Jesus should change our lives in a radical way – just as it did for Peter. The more time we spend with Jesus, the more we will become like Him. Our lives will become polarized and we will stand out from the world.

Our ability to share Jesus comes down ultimately to our closeness with Jesus. What if we saw evangelism as moving someone one step closer to Jesus? It's sharing your story of how Jesus has impacted your life with someone. It's inviting someone into your life and having a conversation with them about your life. Yes, it's important to think through questions like we have posed above- but what if sharing your faith with someone was as easy as sharing your life with someone?

If my life consists of the following slices of life: marriage, kids, job, church, social life, spiritual life, compartmentalizing these significant parts of my life compels me then to evangelize at the expense of other things. Or in other words we may say "I've got to find time to share Jesus." But if I live an integrated life in Jesus, then my ordinary life becomes a life of evangelism because by living daily for Jesus, I am sharing Jesus daily with others.

Here's how I think it works. This means that when you talk about your kids, your marriage, your job, your friends, your church, your passions, you are talking about Jesus. Sharing about the joys in your marriage or your struggles to have a better relationship with your spouse becomes a moment that you can share how Jesus helps you to become a better husband or wife. Your passions to be a designer become a talking point to share how Jesus has given you this passion, and how you want to use your creativity to inspire others about the Creator. Your love of being a father is like the love of God who is a Father; so when you talk about your kids, you can talk about how God loves like a father, too.

I know there will be moments where we have to intentionally engage with others about hard spiritual matters (afterlife, heaven and hell, being born again, God and suffering for example). We absolutely need to have these theological conversations. But the reality we face as the everyday Christian is that sharing Jesus with someone can be overwhelming. But when Jesus becomes your life—is your life—talking about Jesus to others becomes less intimidating and more life-giving. The church in Thessaloniki understood this well, "We were delighted to share with you not only the gospel but our whole lives as well" (1 Thessalonians 2:8).

Bringing people to church to hear about Jesus is one way of sharing Jesus. Bringing the church to the people is another way of spreading the hope of Christ with the world. That's why the church doesn't have to be the only valuable entity for sharing Jesus with the world. You are just as valuable- if not more so.

The New Young Christian is rethinking evangelism.

Here are a few more thoughts to get you inspired to share Jesus more often:

1: HAVE MORE CONVERSATIONS AND FEWER CONFRONTATIONS.

It's a different era now than before. The question of "If you were to die today, do you know where you would go?" was a stirring question because of the Cold War and the nuclear threat which was very real to those who lived during a time of extreme nuclear threat. However, today the engagement with others in your community (your neighborhood, your school, your workplace.) about Christianity is more of an abrasive issue than at any time in history. The idea of being in a "battle" is imagery that is less appealing to both Christians and non-Christians. If we posture ourselves toward a dialogue rather than engaging in a battle for truth, we will most likely be more effective.

2: BEING AN INVITING PERSON IS MORE IMPORTANT THAN BEING A CONVINCING PERSON.

Being convincing is a good thing. But choosing to sacrifice our access to others as an inviting person at the expense of making sure we are convincing enough not only causes us to lose touch with our culture, and it will isolate us as well. If our posture is open with those we are having a conversation with, then usually that is reciprocated and they will be more open with you. Underneath it all, you can and are certain about your faith. But it's not what you should lead with. Because your confidence will come across as arrogance to an outsider of faith. Smugness and superiority in things of faith are not appealing. In contrast, humility and serving go a long way. I think that's why grace is so appealing. Grace is inviting and not imposing. Grace and truth go together (John 1:17). So let grace be the invitation to lead the way, and truth will always back you up when necessary.

3: PASSION IS THE KEY TO A MESSAGE WORTH LISTENING TO.

I have been reading a book titled 'Talk Like Ted', and one of the takeaways from that worthwhile read is that "people cannot inspire others until they are inspired themselves." A genuine passion for Jesus, who He is and what He stands for is critical when sharing authentically with others. But it's a passion for the right thing that is important.

Howard Shultz, founder of Starbucks, wasn't as passionate about coffee as he was about creating a "third space." This is a space that would create incredible customer service, and a place that people would love coming to work where they would be treated with respect. Coffee was the product, but the passion was the care of people (customers and employees). When sharing passionately with others, the focus must remain on the people and not the theology of Christianity.

Jesus was more passionate about loving others and less concerned about religious laws—let that be our model as well.

4: STOP CATEGORIZING PEOPLE.

It's easy for us to put people into categories: unsaved friends, worldly neighbors, secular campus, immoral co-workers. I understand that these are harmless descriptions in most instances, but over time we place ourselves in a position of 'us and them', when God is desiring 'we' and 'family.'

Jesus created meaningful relationships with society's sinners and outcasts. Many Christians, without realizing it, will shame and condescend others by creating a rigid exclusivity. Over time, that can be hard to penetrate by someone who lacks faith.

I personally believe the word 'hope' is one of the most powerful words in our culture, and bringing the hope of Jesus to a world that is severely lacking in hope could be one of the most robust ways to share about Jesus in our culture. The New Young Christian believes peace, hope and forgiveness are potent words that work powerfully in unbelieving contexts.

At my church, River Valley Church, there is a song that we sing that somehow releases an evangelistic heart and passion into our community. It has an unbelievable ability to awaken myself and all of us singing it to the needs that are in our city and in our world. The song is titled "World Needs Jesus." And the lyrics go like this:

When our homes are hit by heartbreak
Let Your presence meet us here
When the pain seems overwhelming
We hold onto You
When the streets are torn by chaos
We will be Your hands and feet
When the darkness brings division
May we be Your light
'Cause we know our world needs Jesus
We know that our world needs freedom
So give us eyes to see the hurting and the broken
And let our lives align with every word You say
When the nations ache from violence
We will be Your blessed peace
When the headlines scream injustice
May we shout Your name!
'Cause we know that our world needs Jesus
We know that our world needs freedom
So give us eyes to see the hurting and the broken
And let our lives align with every word You say!

When you wake up every day on mission to simply live like Jesus, not by categorizing relationships but by seeing others around you as creations of God in need of restoration, then your effectiveness in reaching the world around you will increase more than you realize.

5: LIVE A LIFESTYLE OF GENEROSITY.

Simply put, find ways to be a blessing to others. This not only blesses you and produces incredible fruit in your own life because of your giving, but it shows the world that your actions line up with what you say. It shows that you live what you believe. Saying you're a Christian is one thing, but living it authentically on a daily basis is something else. When we give, we are acting like Jesus. In it's simplest terms, Jesus gave so we could live. When you give so others can experience life, you are like Jesus.

6: CHOOSE INTEGRITY IN ALL CIRCUMSTANCES.

Don't compromise your beliefs. Be honest. Be truthful. Have credibility. Situations happen every day where compromise is not only contemplated but expected. I had a situation in college when I was a server in a restaurant. Every day I would pay for my soup, while most of the other college students just "grabbed a little in a bowl" before their shift. I chose to pay even though after my discount it was under a dollar. Little did I know that my manager saw this and it moved him to make this statement: "Most of my other employees steal from me by taking a small amount of soup without paying, but you choose to pay me for the soup. You're studying at Bible College to be a pastor? Tell me more about the kind of faith you have." I'm proud to say I led him to Christ in the back of the restaurant that day. It's who you are when no one is looking and who you are when everyone is looking that not only defines your faith but speaks a message.

7: MODEL FORGIVENESS.

The ability to forgive quickly and often is one of the most powerful ways to show how Christianity really works. When you model forgiveness you show the world an attribute that is not only rare but healthy and healing for the soul—no matter who they are or what faith they come from. Jesus modeled the ultimate forgiveness by saying these words, "Father forgive them, they know not what they do" (Luke 23:34). That kind of forgiveness, loving your enemies and forgiving quickly, is authentic proof that Jesus is who He says He is. When you forgive with the same intensity as Jesus forgave you, others will see Jesus more clearly than they ever could through you.

8: LIVE VULNERABLY.

Sharing your story or testimony with others lets people know they aren't alone. Sharing the broken parts of your life creates common ground for the gospel to be planted. Knowing your faith is knowing your story. Where Jesus entered, what He has done, and what He continues to do in you and through is powerful for people to hear. How God is revealing Himself to me individually is my testimony. How God is revealing Himself to us corporately (our church) is our message. God's revelation to us has the same effect it had on the disciples from the days of Jesus: "For we cannot help speaking about what we have seen and heard" (Acts 4:20). When you have an authentic, life changing encounter with Christ, sharing the broken parts of your life isn't shameful but hopeful. It tells the person you're with that they also can find healing for their own brokenness.

9: BE EXTREMELY HOSPITABLE.

So you invited someone to church and they didn't accept your invitation. Then why not invite them to your house, make brunch and share Jesus with them while you're at it? Matthew used a meal to introduce his friends to Jesus (Mark 2:14-17). Your pool party, game night, block party, Christmas Tea, Chilli Night, spaghetti dinner, movie premier, baseball Sunday, neighbor night or Super Bowl party could be the moment that your friend gets introduced to Jesus. So invite your friends who love Jesus and let them meet others who don't and see what happens.

God seems to give a healthy community, whose intentions are for the common good of others, restorative power to change the world. The book of Hebrews in the Bible puts it this way :

> And let us consider how we may spur one another on toward love and good deeds, not giving up meeting together, as some are in the habit of doing, but encouraging one another—and all the more as you see the Day approaching (Hebrews 10:24–25).

You and I are our brothers' keeper. We must give thought to how we can help other believers. We must consider the impact of our actions on the faith of others, often surrendering personal freedoms so as not to offend others. This alone provides an excellent reason to gather together so that we can be a blessing to others, encouraging them and taking care that they are standing firm as the day of the Lord approaches. This also provides a mandate for the types of practical ministries that help our churches make a powerful impact on other people's lives such as men's group, women's groups, youth ministries, college ministries, single adult ministries, and marriage retreats, just to name a few.

God wants us to share our faith. How we do it will always depend on who we are, because you are the messenger and message. The more comfortable you are within your own relationship with Jesus, the easier it will be to share it with others.

CHAPTER 7 QUESTIONS

1. Do you agree that it is wrong to share your beliefs with someone of a different faith?

2. What is holding you back from sharing your faith with others?

3. Do you believe that the most powerful apologetic (reason to believe in Jesus) is you? Why or why not?

4. Which one do you value most: reason, respect or relationship? Why?

5. Do you believe there is a correlation between your closeness with Jesus and your sharing Jesus?

6. Read this Scripture and answer the following question:

"We were delighted to share with you not only the gospel but our whole lives as well" (1 Thessalonians 2:8).

Which area of your life is the easiest area to share your faith from? Why?

8

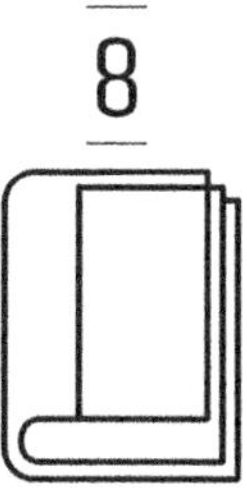

TRUTH-TELLING

LIVING LESS EMOTIONAL AND MORE TRUTHFUL

My son and I were on the edge of the river bank on the St Croix. We decided to yell out the first thing that came to our minds. While my son yelled "Go Vikings!", I yelled "Dad's awesome!" As a matter of fact, it didn't just yell, but it echoed along the riverbanks. I suppose I could've yelled "Jesus is awesome" but apparently I was way to impressed with my hiking skills and leading my son to our father/ son moment that he would cherish for the rest of his life (he doesn't even remember this by the way...I asked him). My son and I realized that what you say (or scream on a river bank) literally impacts what's around you. Literally.

Our echo's were made by our voices bouncing off the other "solids" in nature. That's what an echo is: when a sound is reflected and refracted (or bent) when it collides with something. You then hear the sound repeating itself, getting fainter and fainter as it repeats, bouncing off other objects in its path. Those words my son and I spoke on the banks of the St Croix left our lips and impacted nature and made an echo. The sound waves that came from our voices had real results; and in the same way what we say has an impact. Our words matter because they will make an impact; like telling someone the truth is helpful or telling someone a lie is hurtful.

Words can build people up or tear people down. Words can divide or they can unite. If you have been around the leadership spheres, you have heard this phrase: Words create worlds. What we say about ourselves, about others, and our organizations create the culture that we are living in and leading from. Your words create your conditions and your vernacular creates your environment. As a communicator for a living, I have to listen to what I am saying so that I am creating a community that is life-giving and not self-defeating. As a theologian, I have to be aware of my words and what I am sharing with others because any inaccuracy in what I am saying should be corrected. We do have a responsibility to listen to what is being said and to challenge what is being heard by those around us.

In 2018 Oprah Winfrey received a lifetime achievement award in the 75th Golden Globe Awards. Many people look up to Oprah. She is a shining example of success and a very powerful woman. She is an icon for many women who hope to achieve greatness and become powerful themselves. So when she started to speak about what is a "powerful tool" in her toolbox, many were all ears. In her acceptance speech, she made these comments:

"What I know for sure is that speaking your truth is the most powerful tool we all have…."

The most powerful tool we have is speaking "your truth." Really? Don't get me wrong, Oprah is entertaining and engaging (after all, she is "America's life coach").

But even Oprah can get it wrong. Let me rephrase that. Oprah DID get it wrong, and the "echo" of Oprah's words are still reverberating through the culture: the most powerful tool you have is "my truth."

Think for a moment: Is this a true statement?

Maybe you have already heard or seen these phrases in our culture: "That is my truth," or "know your truth." That phrase before and since Oprah spoke it has been repeated by many and is used to justify a lot of feelings, beliefs and ideas that aren't helpful and in many instances are even more hurtful and harmful to others. As Christians, this phrase is one we cannot keep perpetuating. It seems to be one of those phrases that has caught on, one of those phrases that people use without even knowing why they are using it.

During a time in culture when being tolerant and understanding others is expected, it feels uncomfortable to say "don't speak your truth.'" It seems unacceptable to question this cultural phrase of "speak your truth to power." After all, if this is my truth, shouldn't I be able to speak it? I am writing this to say what if this phrase is NOT truth?

This begs the question, What is truth?

In the Bible, Pontius Pilate asked the question, "What is truth?" (John 18:38). Pontius Pilate was the Roman governor of Judea from A.D. 26-36, serving under Emperor Tiberius. He is most known for his involvement in condemning Jesus to death on a cross. Pontius Pilate is not a fictitious character in the Bible but is mentioned by Tacitus, Philo, and Josephus who were famous historians outside of the Bible. Not only that, the "Pilate Stone," discovered in 1961 and dated c. A.D. 30, includes a description of Pontius Pilate and mentions him as "prefect" of Judea.

Pilate and Jesus came face to face with each other...and with the idea of truth in their modern world. The Gospel of John offers some more detail on this discussion between Pilate and Jesus. Jesus acknowledges Himself not just as a King but as One who also claims to speak directly for the truth:

> "My Kingdom is not an earthly kingdom. If it were, my followers would fight to keep me from being handed over to the Jewish leaders. But my Kingdom is not of this world."
>
> Pilate says, "So you are a king?"
>
> Jesus responds, "You say I am a king. Actually, I was born and came into the world to testify to the truth. All who love the truth recognize that what I say is true."
>
> "What is truth?" Pilate asked." (John 18:38)

Pilate responded with the famous question, "What is truth?" Jesus confirmed what He says to Pilate many times throughout Scripture and most importantly with His famous words found in John 14:6, "I am the Way, the Truth and the Life. No one comes to the Father except through Me." (John 14:6)

Jesus is the truth. The Bible is the truth. Jesus always spoke the truth. Jesus and the Bible both continually tell the truth about God, about man, and about evil (John 1:1,14). As Christians, we are meant to communicate the truth of Jesus Christ to a hurting and broken world; and not just a world in chaos, but a world under the influence of a personal enemy that is constantly affecting us, hurting us and lying to us. Because if Jesus is the source of truth, then there must be a source of lies as well. Where is this deceptive source?

Well, there is an enemy that stands in opposition to the truth and to everything we do and represent as Christians. This enemy is named in the Scriptures as the devil. The devil is known for a lot of things and is named as a lot of things in the Bible; the enemy (Matthew 13:39), Satan (Revelation 12:9, 20:2), the devil (Matthew 4:1, 5, 8, 11, 9:32), the accuser (Revelation 12:10)- to name a few. But one more name for the opposition to our soul which is important to consider within the context of our conversation on truth is "the father of lies" (John 8:44).

A quick study on the devil reveals to us that he was originally called Lucifer, a reference that occurs only in Isaiah 14:12. Lucifer means "morning star." Lucifer, before receiving one of the many names listed above (e.g. devil), was one of several created spirit beings in a class of angels known as Cherubim (Ezekiel 28:14). His initial responsibility was to cover God's throne. When Lucifer rebelled against his Creator, God rejected him and cast him from heaven (Isaiah 12:12-15). An angel that was once one of the most beautiful and honored in heaven, with one of the most sacred privileges in heaven, becomes one of the most ugly and dishonored in heaven.

After the fall of Lucifer, God then makes man. Man's purpose as one of God's premier creations is to oversee creation and to rule over everything.

This is confirmed in the Scripture passage below:

> What are mere mortals that you should think about them, human beings that you should care for them? Yet you made them only a little lower than God and crowned them with glory and honor. You gave them charge of everything you made, putting all things under their authority (Psalm 8:4-6).

So who we call our enemy, and all of his legions of fallen angels, were cast out of heaven (About 1/3 were cast out of heaven and joined Lucifer in this rebellion Revelation 12:4). Lucifer, the devil, will now stop at nothing and will do anything to bring as many of humankind with him.

Why am I expounding on this story specifically? Because Lucifer is named by God in the Bible as the "father of lies." Because one of the greatest threats to the truth of salvation and our eternity with Jesus is the lies of the enemy. The Bible gives us a snapshot into this conversation between man and the devil in the Garden of Eden. Man had to make a choice between believing God's words or the devil's. One source was the Father of Truth and the other source was the father of lies. We can relate to those moments when we have had a choice to listen to the words spoken by God from the Bible or the words spoken by the enemy through the cultural outlets around us. For example, mankind believed a lie instead of the truth. When Adam and Eve rejected God's truth and accepted the devil's lie, that was the moment that all the troubles of the whole world began.

You have the same option.

When you are faced with a decision, to make a judgment call, to decide on a moral dilemma, you have the same ultimatum to discover: is this a truth or a lie? Siding with truth will always confirm Jesus, His will and His future for your life. The opposite is also true. Whenever you do the opposite of what Jesus says, you side with the devil's lies instead of God's truth.

We have a sinful nature and that sinful nature compels us to drift toward the words of our enemy rather than the wisdom of Jesus. We'd rather believe the devil's lie than God's truth. But Jesus wasn't afraid to call Satan what he is: a liar and the father of lies! Jesus said, "There is no truth in him. When he speaks a lie, he speaks from his own resources, for he is a liar and the father of it" (John 8:44).

Again, if the opposite of truth is a "lie" then it makes sense that if Jesus is the ultimate truth-teller then the devil is the ultimate "lie -carrier." This again begs the question: in a world of opinions, fake news, 'my truth', and deception from both the natural and supernatural realms, what is truth? Jesus said, "You shall know the truth, and the truth shall make you free" (John 8:32).

He said, "I am the truth." Jesus did not say, "You shall know a truth" or "any truth" but "THE truth." He's the embodiment of all truth. Jesus said, "If you do not believe that I am He, you will die...." (John 8:24). If you don't believe what Jesus says and don't accept Him, the truth is that you will die in your sins and you'll be lost. The ultimatum is huge. There's so much at stake in this life—and the next—when you listen to the words of Jesus and choose to believe them. In a world that is adopting the idea that we are free to believe, speak and live from "my truth," are we willing to face the truth?

An example to help us as we consider the importance of THE truth over MY truth can be found in Paul. Paul was a theologian in his day who cared deeply about sharing his ways of life and faith. He held onto it so tightly and believed so much in preserving his "theological point of view" that Paul would say: Believe in "my truth" or be killed. The choice is yours.

Paul came face to face with Jesus and exchanged "this personal truth" of his for "the truth" that Jesus died and was resurrected. Paul's revelation of who Jesus was and what He was doing made him a believer and a carrier of "the truth" of Jesus. That truth became "my gospel" in the Scriptures for Paul.

Consider this Scripture, "Remember Jesus Christ, raised from the dead, descended from David. This is my gospel" (2 Timothy 2:8).

He was personally impacted by the gospel. The Gospel or the "Good News" of Jesus Christ was carried deeply and held tightly by Paul to the end of his life. But unlike "my truth," the phrase "my gospel" was not a phrase about Paul's ability. It was not a maxim about his own self-reliance. He was not declaring a path just for himself. Let's silence the echo of the fake truths in our lives and shout from the top of our lungs the Good News of a good God who has a good future for us all. Because that's MY GOSPEL and the truth!

Here are four ways that will help you to live less emotional and more truthful:

1: DECIPHER THE DIFFERENCE BETWEEN TRUTH AND OPINION.

Truth is a powerful concept. When you hold a belief as a truth it can be a source of strength, motivation, even comfort. But there is a difference between truth and opinion. Here are a few:

- Truth refers to something that can be verified vs. opinion which refers to judgments or beliefs about something.
- Truth is shown with unbiased words vs opinions are expressed with bias words.
- Truth is objective reality vs opinion is a subjective statement.
- Truth is universal vs opinion differs from person to person.

While there are multiple ways to express the truth, there is still only one truth. Declaring something as "my truth" gives the inaccurate and unhelpful perception that truth is changing. When truth is not a constant and inevitable reality we must respond to, it doesn't help us but hurts us as we are left without anything consistent or trustworthy on which to stand upon.

For example we build our whole mathematical system on the fact that 2 + 2 = 4. We may want it to be more.

We feel it should be more. But it will never, ever, equal 5. Just because I insist something is true for me or "my truth," it does not mean it is "the truth." I can hope for it, believe it and want it to be true, but there is the chance it could just be my opinion, my suggestion or my feeling.

2: START DESIRING GOD'S TRUTH INSTEAD OF DESIGNING YOUR OWN.

There have been plenty of times in my life when I have believed something as true for me but it was not actually true, even though I wished it was. It was my design; or even worse…the design of my parents.

Like Santa Claus.

There was once a time when I was emphatic that Santa Claus was real. No matter how much I was sure this jolly saint was sneaking into my house with presents, there came the reality check when I was in 5th grade (I was a late believer) that it was a lie. My parents finally told me the truth. I told the guys at my lunch table they were lying to me when they said the source of my presents was my parents. I emphatically said, "So my parents are magically going all over the world giving presents to you and all the kids in the world? Really Jason? Yeah-I don't think so!" I mean sure, my dad was slightly overweight, but to have the superpower of making animals fly and travel at 5,083,000 mph to ensure presents are delivered by morning was not just crazy…it would've been a dream come true! So I went home that day after school and confronted my parents and finally heard the shocking truth. Santa Claus was a lie.

And no matter how much I believed Santa was the one putting a few presents under the tree for my brother and I, it was always "my truth" but it was never "the truth." No matter how much we believe something to be true, it might be a design of our own.

The desire to hold to "my truth" is not a new desire. Like Adam and Eve in the Garden, we can insist and believe it is our right to eat from the tree of knowledge of good and evil. We have the mental capacity as grown men and women to decide what is right and good and what is not. But by doing so, we place ourselves in the position of defining truth. We are not the creators of truth, and we should not act (or speak) as if we are. As Christians we believe that He is the truth. As Christians we must be consumed with His truth and not our own.

"Half-truth" is also an interesting word we have created in our culture. It's a word that we have designed. A half truth is "a statement that is only partly true, especially one intended to deceive, evade blame, or the like; a statement that fails to divulge the whole truth."

A half of a truth is like watching 1/2 of a movie and leaving in the middle. I think films are modern day parables. I think the movie theater is on many occasions the modern day "stained glass window" telling us stories about forgiveness, redemption and love (with of course some great CGI and amazing fight scene choreography). But what I hate is leaving a film in the middle. I have NEVER done it. Even if it's a bad film. I can't leave and walk out in the middle of it. I can't. I have to know what happens. Because I don't like the thought of imagining what could have happened to the character when there was an intended end by the storyteller and I chose to leave. There is an intended result. The script is written. The story is crafted and the ending is certain. But I choose to believe it up to a point and then pull out when I don't like what's happening.

Life can be the same way. We are tempted to believe up to a point, then fill in the blanks with our own ideas and craft our own ending. But the story of Jesus and the Scriptures assure us that there is an ending that belongs to us all and that finale is secure in Jesus who is the author, perfecter and finisher of our faith (Hebrews 12:2).

What I love about being a Christian is that I don't have the pressure or the confusion to build my life on "my truth." This gives me freedom! I am free from the stress of trying to make my purpose. I am free from trying to figure out what happens after I die. I am free from constructing my own fragile reality when God has shown me what real life is like through the lens of Scripture. I am free from figuring out what my future could be with my own limited knowledge and understanding, and all I have to do is surrender and trust the God who knows every day of life before I have ever lived it (Psalm 139:16).

3: STOP LIVING ACCORDING TO HOW YOU FEEL BECAUSE IT'S NOT ALWAYS TRUE.

Facts and feelings are at odds on a regular basis. But feelings can't be the driving force behind our decisions, our actions and our beliefs. Reshaping your life around your feelings will result in a fragile life that can switch direction on a dime. Life was never meant to be built on the fragility of emotions. Because how you feel is not always how you are or who you are. If my feelings line up to what the truth of my situation is...then those moments are treasured, valid and can be trusted. But we have to be mature enough to differentiate when my feelings aren't in alignment. True life is meant to be lived by embracing the truth- even when it's uncomfortable and doesn't feel good. God's truth always helps us to understand the complex reality of the world we live in, which is essential to functioning as a human.

4: BUILD A SECOND OPINION CIRCLE.

It's easy to get it wrong. How do I know this? I've stood in front of a mirror, looked at myself and said "dang, I look good." Then, within that same 10 second window, my wife walks by and says "are you wearing that?" I thought my hotness level was at a 10. According to her, I didn't even register on the scale. So I changed and am now realizing she loves my personality and not always my fashion choices.

Some people do not want any advice. Some people listen to only "one kind" of advice. Some are very open to peers. Some are adverse to the counsel of older people. Some of us are only open to the opinions of people who are of our own economic level, our own race, gender or political persuasion. The power of advice though in a person's life is it can change your life. And not just change your life but advance your life.

The "Christian walk" is about forward motion. It's about getting to places that God has ordained for you and that will unlock your future. It's about moving forward towards what God has for you. And this will require you to make decisions that will move you closer spiritually, financially, relationally, emotionally into God's will for your life. The decisions you make can move your forward or can move you backward.

A university study at Cornell found out that the average adult will make around 35,000 decisions a day. We are bombarded by decisions we have to make each day. Some of these decisions are easy and some are hard— and they can paralyze us. We call this "deciding not to decide." You've experienced this when your friend says "where do you wanna eat?" and you respond with "I don't care, you decide." You didn't want to use up "brain power" to think about a decision that had little to do with what you were accomplishing that day, so you chose NOT to decide and to put it in the hands of your friends. Some indecisions are small (like Chick-fil-A or Popeyes - Chick fil-A, duh!), while others are far greater like breaking off a relationship, deciding to change careers, or moving into a new house. Choosing to not decide can result in you getting stuck in life, while taking the risk and making a choice can help you thrive in life and survive.

While we can become overwhelmed to the point of even indecision, let's take Bear Grylls advice on making decisions to survive, "Survival is about being fearless. It's about making a decision, getting on and doing it..."

Essentially Bear Grylls is saying that if you want to

survive in life, you are going to have to make decisions. Those decisions will move you forward or backward—and you can make them based on emotion or truth. Just like needing Bear to give us a kick in the butt, we need people to help us to see through the cloud of emotion and indecision, and make God led decisions based on the truth.

We need a "second opinion circle."

What is a second opinion circle? It's a group of people that you trust that can give context, advice and a second opinion on the decision you have to make. They help you discover the truth about a situation and they will help you realize if you are living emotionally or truthfully. They can help you decipher between opinion and truth. If you're going to make good decisions, you need other people to be involved in your life. You're going to need a community that can help filter your thoughts, feelings and ideas that you have. To not have this, according to the Bible, is foolish. Solomon, known in antiquity and the Scriptures as the wisest man who ever lived, gave this advice when trying to make decisions:

> "For lack of guidance a nation falls but victory is won through many advisers" (Proverbs 11:14).

> "Whoever walks with the wise becomes wise but the companion of fools suffer harm" (Proverbs 13:20).

> "Plans fail for lack of counsel but with many advisers they succeed" (Proverbs 15:22).

> "Surely you need guidance to wage war and victory is won through many advisers" (Proverbs 24:6).

It comes down to this singular question: "Are you willing to suspend your own truth about what you believe about your situation and submit it to someone else to speak into it? Someone who is trusted, wiser, and committed to seeing you get to the best place that you need to be in life?" This question is hard for many of us. I think the reason it is hard is because we have lost confidence in the institutions, authorities and other sources of cultural credibility that once held a higher value. Our parents, police, president and other voices that were once trusted and truthful voices, have diminished in their reliability and their authority. So we choose to distance ourselves from them. And when we distance ourselves from other voices, we tend to do it on our own.

But God has designed all of us to have community and covering. While no one is perfect, God desires you to have a group of people you can trust, that believe in you and are helping you advance farther in life and deeper in God—and to live a life of truth. In the Bible, Peter is speaking and inspiring those in his Biblical community to do the same. Peter writes it this way:

> In the same way, you who are younger, submit yourselves to your elders. All of you, clothe yourselves with humility toward one another, because 'God opposes the proud but shows favor to the humble.'

Humble yourselves, therefore, under God's mighty hand, that he may lift you up in due time (1 Peter 5:5-6).

Being a New Young Christian means that no matter what season of life you are in, there is someone else who has lived through it. That person is typically wiser and more experienced than you. The word "elder" referenced above in the Scripture is a word that is used for those who are not just older, but those who have lived through where you need to go. They are farther along in the journey than you. The verse referenced above says that we are not only to be in proximity to elders, but we are to submit to them.

For example, if you are wanting to go college or start your own business, find that person you trust that has started their own business and ask them about the difficulties. Talk to someone who has been married for a few years and ask about the challenges of having a spouse. Find another mom who has lived through the "baby stage" of life and let them tell you about the "life hacks" of navigating the season. Find someone who has gone off to college and have them talk about the difficulties of staying connected to God while being away from home. Talk to someone who quit their job to try a different field and find out that it's not as easy as it looks. While finding older people you can trust is important, it's less about age and more about experience. A second opinion circle has voices in it that are trusted by you who have gone ahead of you, in years and experience, to tell you what the terrain is like, where the path can be difficult, and the places along your journey to avoid and how to get to where they are.

God shows us in the verse we read earlier that the hardest part of this will be your pride. Pride is subtle. It can be hard to detect in your life. But you can tell there is pride in your life when you have said these things:

- I don't need someone to open the door for me to get a job, I can do this on my own.
- I just feel like I won't like it, so why bother trying.
- I don't need my parents to tell me what to do.
- Everyone says he's not right for me, but they don't know him like I do and I know he loves me..
- I just feel like I need to do this for me and you don't get me.

Pride is essentially saying: you can do it yourself. That you don't need community or covering. That's why humility is necessary when building your second opinion circle. It's admitting that you CAN'T DO IT ALONE and that others are necessary. It's admitting that you don't have all the answers and that others do. It's inviting others into your decision-making process and asking them to speak into your current situation; and not just those who agree with you but those who want the best for you. That is humility and when you humble yourself, you are lifted up to the places that God always had in mind for you!

How do you build a "Second Opinion Circle?"

1: BE A TEACHABLE PERSON.

Being teachable means that you are capable of receiving instruction. Teachability is an attitude that will never stop learning. Pastor and author Matt Keller says it is "Being willing to relearn what we think we already know." Early on as leaders many of us are teachable because we are new. However, the more successful we become, the less teachable we become. The Rich Young Ruler was successful professionally, personally and spiritually (Matthew 19:16-22). He was influential, with many speaking about him, but with no one speaking into him. Jesus encounters this young adult. He looked at him, loved him and corrected him:

> Jesus answered, "If you want to be perfect, go, sell your possessions and give to the poor, and you will have treasure in heaven. Then come, follow me." When the young man heard this, he went away sad, because he had great wealth (Matthew 19:21-22).

When Jesus pointed out a flaw in his path to success, he resisted. He walked away sad and essentially missing out on following Jesus (maybe even being one of the 12 disciples!). Who has permission in your life to tell you the truth, even when things seem to be going great for you?

2: REALIZE YOUR FRIENDS AREN'T ALWAYS RIGHT.

Even though you may have friends who give you their opinions, they aren't always right. While we love our friends, they don't always give the best advice. You've experienced it when they have the day off the next day and want you to call in sick for work. Or they make you go to that movie that "everyone's talking about" and you find yourself sitting there thinking, "this is 2 hours I won't get back and $12 I will never see again." Or they make you try that "amazing hole-in-the-wall" that you knew didn't look like the safest place to eat but they "heard it has the best nacho's," leaving you questioning your life choices as you are bowing down and worshipping "the porcelain god" in the bathroom. You shouldn't have listened to them.

Rehoboam, a young man taking on the new position of king, knew this pressure. When becoming king, he had his group of friends giving him advice on some decisions he should make during his first week in office. Then there were those that have been around a while. They were elders who offered him advice on how they thought he should lead. They lived under the rule of Rehoboam's father, King Solomon, and had been around the block a few times when it came to living in the kingdom and living under the previous administration. They also had advice on how this new, young king should rule. Which counsel would he choose? King Rehoboam's decision is chronicled in the Bible in the book of 1 Kings:

> Then King Rehoboam consulted the elders who had served his father Solomon during his lifetime. "How would you advise me to answer these people?" he asked. They replied, "If today you will be a servant to these people and serve them and give them a favorable answer, they will always be your servants." But Rehoboam rejected the advice the elders gave him and consulted the young men who had grown up with him and were serving him (1 Kings 12:6-8).

Rehoboam chose his friends. He should've listened to the advice of the elders in the kingdom. He chose wrong and it cost him. Listening to the advice of his friends was not only short-sighted but it was devastating as it ultimately divided the kingdom in half! His circle didn't have people in it who thought differently. They were living in an "illusion of invulnerability." His circle of friends made this new king and all of those in the circle feel invincible. And that was the illusion. They weren't. The lesson here: find people who are outside of your normal thinking, age and expertise. Invite them in to give you their perspective. It may help you avoid some very big missteps!

3: FIND PEOPLE FARTHER THAN YOU.

Find the people around you who are modeling where you want to go. Find people who have gone before you and have walked through your life stage to coach you through it. Find someone who is similar in strengths and personality as you and ask them how they have dealt with the personality traits that can sabotage. A mentor represents the direction you want to go in and who you want to become. I've spent a lot of time trying to intentionally pursue friendships and relationships with people who are smarter, more skilled and simply 'better' than me. Faithfulness celebrates progress more than success. Find people who didn't give up. Look for people who chose to go the distance.

> For this reason I have sent to you Timothy, my son whom I love, who is faithful in the Lord. He will remind you of my way of life in Christ Jesus, which agrees with what I teach everywhere in every church (1 Corinthians 4:17).

This relationship between Paul and Timothy is a mentorship relationship that has had a ripple effect throughout the New Testament. Timothy came from a single parent home. He didn't have a father but had a mom who loved God and helped her son discover faith. When you are a follower of Jesus but are without a father, God will always fill in that gap with Biblical community, other men and women in the church who will mentor you, coach you and inspire you to be better and to do more. Timothy needed Paul's opinion and advice in his own spiritual life, and the result is he becomes someone who not only had a father in the faith, but a successful pastor, taking over congregations that Paul planted in his missionary journey. Timothy was humble enough to realize he needed a man of God in his life and was vulnerable enough to trust him and God was faithful enough to give Paul to him.

Before this, Paul didn't just wake up an "awesome Christian" one day. He also had a man who mentored him, Barnabus. His name means "encourager." To encourage means to "in-courage" or in other words to put "courage in" someone. Barnabus mentored Paul for a few years in the desert as he was growing in his own faith. The point: great leaders have great mentors. Great fathers have great fathers. Great mothers have great mothers. Someone along their journey has showed them who they are and where they need to go. These "sons and daughters in the faith" didn't do it on their own. They didn't choose to believe "their truth" but followed "the truth" into a future that blesses them in return. Truth-tellers are born because they are "truth-seekers" and seeking after wisdom and counsel is one of the most important decisions you can make as The New Young Christian.

CHAPTER 8 QUESTIONS

1. How have you seen the difference of "the truth" and "my truth" in your own life?

2. How does knowing there is an outside influence affecting some of your decisions (the devil) make you think about the choices you are currently making?

3. Do you feel you've designed your own truth in certain situations? Explain.

4. How has the misalignment of truth and feelings affected you in your life when it came to following Jesus?

5. Is it hard to find people that you trust in your life to give you advice?

6. Which Proverb inspires you the most and why during the "Second Opinion Circle" portion?

7. Why is both "community" and "covering" important?

8. Do you have a father/mother in the faith? Why or why not? Do you think it's necessary?

9

PEACEMAKING

LOVING LIKE JESUS IN A TOLERANT AND POLITICAL CULTURE

There is a rise of outrage today in culture. Outrage is exhausting. It's draining. Outrage can take a psychological and physical toll on us. Yet it seems we can't live without it. It's become similar to an addiction. On some level people enjoy getting outraged; it makes them feel that they're on the right side. It helps them feel that they are bonding with others who have similar views. But is it really bonding? Uniting over your disdain for someone still doesn't feel right.

Maybe because it's not right.

We live in a culture where anything you say can be misconstrued and someone will take offense to it. Once that individual or group speaks out, the public mob is out to put your head on a spike. It's eroding our interactions, our relationships and our society. When a group of people are continually in "outrage mode" it's very unhealthy. Heather Wilhelm, in an article for the Chicago Tribune writes:

> For a frightening number of people, the art of being offended by everything—or, even better, loudly and publicly complaining about being offended by everything—is pursued with alarming dedication. For some, being offended is practically a credo and an all-encompassing way of life.

There is a difference between participating in a culture of outrage and having firm convictions. Jesus calls Christians to respond differently to a hateful world, commanding us to refuse retaliation and instead extend grace to our enemies. This is a different ethic than what we are used to, but Jesus modeled it. Jesus lived with a completely different set of standards.

The Sermon on the Mount is perhaps the most famous portion of Scripture in the Bible. Specifically in this sermon Jesus lays out a completely different manner of living for His disciples. It's a way of life that is counter-cultural to the world's mentality and emotions. In His sermon, Jesus instructs His disciples on how to deal with a world that is antagonistic, unwelcoming, mean-spirited and wants to take advantage of them. And His simple instruction is this: Turn the other cheek.

Matthew followed Jesus as one of His disciples. He heard all of the sermons and was there when Jesus was preaching His famous Sermon on the Mount. Matthew recorded Jesus words from the sermon here:

> You have heard that it was said, 'An eye for an eye, and a tooth for a tooth.' But I say to you, do not resist an evil person; but whoever slaps you on your right cheek, turn the other to him also. If anyone wants to sue you and take your shirt, let him have your coat also. Whoever forces you to go one mile, go with him two. Give to him who asks of you, and do not turn away from him who wants to borrow from you (Matthew 5:38–42).

The Jewish law created equity with this "eye for an eye" ruling, which was a common rule that was around and spoken in the Jewish community for centuries. It dates back and originates from the Code of Hammurabi. It is found in the Old Testament books of Exodus and Leviticus and its meaning in the Bible was simply this: the punishment or sentencing should equally match the crime. But the purpose of the law was never to give license to inflict as much pain on someone as you thought they had inflicted upon you. So Jesus, instead, calls His followers to a completely different standard in their personal dealings with others. While the Jewish law was concerned with people's actions, Jesus' commands surpass a person's actions and goes far deeper... into the person's heart. Instead of using the law as an excuse for personal vengeance, Jesus commands those who are citizens of His kingdom to refuse retaliation when treated poorly. His advice was "turn the other cheek." As hard as that would be for any of us, it's a simple phrase that reflects an attitude that says, "while we may not agree on what you are saying and doing, I'm going to resist retaliating and choose forgiving."

"I'm going to keep my words to a minimum and try to see things from your perspective."

In an "outrage culture", sometimes silence can speak louder than yelling back. Raising your voice often places undeserved importance on the object of our outrage. Before long, our priorities can become as distorted as those of the broader culture. And when that happens, we start to believe our "narrative of offense." The result is we spend our time fighting for the wrong things.

There are times to be furious. You can be "angry and not sin" (Ephesians 4:26). Probably one of the best examples of this is when Jesus flipped tables in the temple. After making His triumphal entry into Jerusalem with crowds cheering and palm branches waving, Jesus "went into the temple and began to drive out those who bought and sold in it" (Luke 19:45–46).

Was Jesus showing the first signs of "outrage culture?" Hardly. It was righteous indignation. Why such a display of anger? Because the people engaged in temple commerce were keeping others from God. They had a "financial racket" going. They were finding fault with the sacrificial animals the people brought in and then sold them as an "approved" animal, at an inflated price. This made Jesus angry. If you're a normal human, that should make you angry. As Christians, we should speak out against injustice, but there is a difference between speaking out against injustice and "lashing out" in a Twitter fight where two different camps of people belittle each other in order to try and prove their point. Refusing to retaliate is NOT an excuse to be passive or avoid people. Jesus' words are not a call to disengage. They are a command to "turn the other cheek" and "go the extra mile" instead.

It was common under Roman occupation during Jesus' day for soldiers to demand that citizens carry their pack. This is what Jesus had in mind in Matthew when he told His followers to go that extra mile. For this idea to have its full effect, we must remember Roman soldiers were part of an occupying authority. They were an oppressive political power, and one that many Jews were desiring to overthrow. In fact, several attempts had already been made in Jesus' day to start a rebellion against the Romans. Roman soldiers were known to strike Jews to show their strength, and abuse their power to enforce their authority and Caesar's rule and reign over others.

But Jesus tells His disciples to do something counter-cultural concerning the opposing political party. If struck, they were to not strike back in revolt. Not only that, they were to submit to the request to carry the Roman soldiers pack by exceeding the expected distance. Do not just do what is expected of you to fulfill the obligation, Jesus tells them, instead do something that can only be explained by genuine love for the person doing you wrong. Instead of returning insult for insult, go out of your way to return kindness instead. Instead of getting drawn into the outrage, let us live a better story.

I'm fully aware that it's not easy. It's especially hard when we have those in charge over us that we don't agree with politically, socially, relationally, spiritually.

So, how do we honor those God has put in our lives when we don't agree with them?

Honoring those we don't agree with.

1: STOP LABELING EACH OTHER AND START LEARNING FROM EACH OTHER.

Christians can fall into the trap of dishonoring others whose political beliefs or ideas are different than theirs. Left-leaning Christians engage in rhetoric that labels our right-leaning authorities as anti-poor, anti-women, anti-immigrant and so on. Right-leaning Christians can label our democratic friends on the left as anti-capitalist, anti-white, anti-baby, anti-cop. What if we labeled each other as human beings? What if we saw each other as creations of God? That label gives us a starting point to engage with others that isn't political, but personal to God. It gives us permission to accept each other despite our political positions, so we can listen to each other rather than scream at each other. Pursue the right perspective of each other before pursuing the right to push back against each other.

2: BEING DISAGREEABLE DOESN'T MEAN BEING DISHONORABLE.

When the actions of those in authority disagree with your view of what leaders should do, you have a choice to make. Young David, an up-and-coming leader, became successful and did everything right with those around him, even with those who were in authority over him. King Saul, a political and spiritual leader to whom David reported, chose to be irrational and dysfunctional to the point of wanting to kill David. How would you honor a man who relentlessly sought to kill you?

David had an understanding that God puts kings in charge, and he knew that God had established Saul as king (1 Samuel 9:15–16). Every response by David toward Saul's rants revealed to others how much David loved God, by how much he honored Saul. David spared Saul's life in the cave (1 Samuel 24:4–22) and again on the field of war while Saul was sleeping (1 Samuel 26:1–12). While there were many chances to "pay back" this ruler and his administration, David chose a different path. He surrendered his heart, his conviction and his opinions of this irrational ruler to God. Eventually Saul was defeated in battle against his enemies and fell upon his own sword. And it should be noted, David not only grieved his death, he prayed, he fasted, and even wrote a song about his fallen leader (2 Samuel 1:17–27). How's that for a "cheek turn!" Instead of recounting all of Saul's weaknesses, the song he wrote actually recounted his honor. Whenever possible, show respect for those in charge no matter how crazy they can be or sound (and maybe even write a song about them!).

3: ENGAGE WITH MATURITY.

It's hard when we don't get our own way. My kids have taught me that. When they were younger, they attempted to throw a tantrum, hit and scream. That behavior didn't last long because that's what immaturity fosters. But maturity provokes civility, conversation and peaceful discourse. Often, when we choose to riot, rebel and resist, it communicates a message to others that we are immature. God wants us though to be mature as Christians—not just mature, but "Christlike." Peter puts it like this:

> For God called you to do good, even if it means suffering, just as Christ suffered for you. He is your example, and you must follow in his steps. He never sinned, nor ever deceived anyone. He did not retaliate when he was insulted, nor threaten revenge when he suffered. He left his case in the hands of God, who always judges fairly (1 Peter 2:21–23).

It's tempting to bully or launch a text you will regret from behind the keyboard on your phone. But it would be far more valuable to organize your thoughts, take a deep breath, compose yourself, find empathy and bless that person and steward the conversation well. Many people feel like they can't get involved because they don't know where to start. Just find a door of opportunity and start the conversation.

4: INSTEAD OF CREATING WALLS, CREATE OPPORTUNITIES.

Jesus chose to go into difficult places, not avoid them. He was seen with the marginalized, the broken and the hurting. He was a friend of drunks, sexual deviants and outcasts. He was more pro-woman than any political figure in history considering the context of the first century. He was more "politically right" with His beliefs about Scripture, loving the religious, supporting the Roman military and leading with charity. He also was more "politically left" with the way He chose to love: Jesus fed the hungry, reached out cross-culturally, identified with the poor, loved the religious and fought for the outsider. He chose to live by breaking down walls. When we break down walls and come together with those who are different than we are, we show the world that we are His disciples and that Jesus is who He said He is.

5: LIVE IN THE "IN-BETWEEN."

The "in-between" is that space between the extremes of faith and politics. Here's what I mean. Take Matthew and Simon. These are two of Jesus' disciples. Jesus recruited Simon the Zealot (essentially an anti-government radical) to be on his team while also recruiting Matthew (a Roman government employee). Jesus showed us all that two people on polar opposites of the political spectrum can live and love in community together. We will always be surrounded by these two sides: those who "share my faith but don't agree with my politics" and those who "share my political view but don't agree with my faith." How you live in the in-between is a big indicator of your own heart. If Jesus can do it, so can you.

6: PUMP THE BRAKES ON CONDITIONAL HONORING.

We are quick to dismiss others who don't agree with our political views, parenting views, etc. We seem to have drifted into a conversational norm of "I will respect you if you respect me, but if we disagree then forget you!" People are going to disagree with you. Simply writing them off and calling them a name, or putting a label on them, doesn't make us better as a community. Just because you don't agree with them doesn't mean they aren't human. God wants us to honor all people (1 Peter 2:17). Honor is not an emotional response, but rather is meant to be a humble response. Even Jesus who was being dishonored by everyone around him—He who was deserving of honor but received none—chose the higher road, and we should too. Jesus was remembered this way by the Philippian Church:

> Don't be selfish; don't try to impress others. Be humble, thinking of others as better than yourselves. Don't look out only for your own interests, but take an interest in others, too. You must have the same attitude that Christ Jesus had. Though he was God, he did not think of equality with God as something to cling to. Instead, he gave up his divine privileges; he took the humble position of a slave and was born as a human being, he humbled himself in obedience to God and died a criminal's death on a cross. Therefore, God elevated him to the place of highest honor and gave him the name above all other names (Philippians 2:3–9).

7: SUBMISSION TO AUTHORITIES, NOT SUBVERSION OF AUTHORITIES.

Imagine being forced to live under political leadership you didn't vote for and completely despised. Some of us would say, "Lived it for 8 years under the last President" and some would say "Living it right now with this President." In the book of Daniel, four young and ambitious leaders found themselves living and working under an administration that was different than what they believed in. The administration was enforcing rules that were against the convictions they held. Rather than rebelling and resisting, these young people took a different approach. They honored their leadership in regard to the expectations, the rules and regulations they didn't agree with:

> [Daniel] asked the chief of staff for permission not to eat these unacceptable foods. Now God had given the chief of staff both respect and affection for Daniel. ... Whenever the king consulted them in any matter requiring wisdom and balanced judgment, he found them 10 times more capable (Daniel 1:8–9, 20).

Daniel chose outreach over outrage. He chose to be prophetic instead of political. He chose to stay engaged with his leaders even when it was difficult. The result of responding the right way gave them more political and relational clout than they ever could have imagined. Instead of just protesting and screaming at the sky, what if we chose to have rational discourse with those in charge over us?

We may have the right to protest, but is it the right thing to do right now?

8: PUT YOURSELF IN SOMEONE ELSE'S SHOES.

You probably don't know what it's like to be going through what they are going through. We don't know what's happening behind the scenes. So do your best to gain understanding. That's wisdom according to God, "The beginning of wisdom is: Acquire wisdom; And with all your acquiring, get understanding" (Proverbs 4:7).

So try to understand where the other is coming from. This will not only build a bridge, but will help calm the stormy waters of outrage as you empathize.

9: BEFORE YOU SAY IT, PRAY IT.

I'm guilty of just speaking what I'm feeling. Before you engage with someone or in something, give it some time in prayer. It's there you will get God's heart for your situation and for that person. It's a lot easier for you to see where they are coming from when you see how God sees them.

10: GAIN UNDERSTANDING.

Conflict is often rooted in misunderstanding about where others around you are coming from. When a conflict arises rather than trying to gain understanding, we are often trying to win the argument. Stephen Covey speaks to this in '7 Habits of Highly Effective People' when he says: "Seek first to understand, then to be understood." So guard yourself against assuming. If you're going to assume something, assume the best about that person and not the worst. When you believe the best about someone, you can't help but draw closer to them and draw from them.

11: PRACTICE PEACEMAKING.

That means you need to be intentional to bring peace to people, places and discussions. This is not a peace that is fabricated, but a peace that is faith-related. This is a peace that is not manipulated with the right circumstance, but a peace that is magnified as a person. This is a supernatural peace, a godly peace, that has nothing to do with human beings or human circumstances. In fact, it can't be produced by anyone, but it can be found by everyone. This peace is a person. It's Jesus. He is called the Prince of Peace. So the closer you are to Jesus, the closer you are to peace. Jesus doesn't get stressed out, worried or get afraid, but lives in perfect contentment. You can too. Not only that, but you carry that same peace in you. So when you walk into a room, you bring the peace of Jesus into your boardroom, your classroom, your living room. Practicing peacemaking is easier than you think.

12: HAVE CONVERSATIONS, NOT CONFRONTATIONS.

We've seen enough confrontation to last us a lifetime. So let's start having conversations. That means it is a two-sided dialogue. So be a potent listener. Listening shows more power and grace than you can imagine. We have to listen in order to be listened to, which means don't come into the argument simply telling me what to think or what you think, but ask me what I think. How you say it is just as important as what you say. Don't see barriers but opportunities. Choose to rally around themes that can do the most good: love, honor, peace, humility, kindness, forgiveness and hope. The best conversations begin with showing an interest in the other person, their world, and what they might be interested in. Most people love to talk about themselves. Ask them an open-ended question about something that you notice about them. If you can give them a sincere compliment or give them positive feedback, you've made a great start. Great conversationalists have a sincere interest in others, notice things about them, and use these things to start and fuel their conversations.

13: BE A GOOD NEIGHBOR.

I know we already said it, but we can't say it enough: Love God and love your neighbor as yourself. True joy is not found in pursuing our own desires, but fulfilling the desires of others. So we choose to keep our doors open and our lives open as good neighbors to create a better community. Acceptance is more palatable to culture than resistance, so we choose to accept people where they are and influence people toward Jesus. So we follow the advice of the Bible, "Let us think of ways to motivate one another to acts of love and good works." (Hebrews 10:24)

At the end of the day, isn't it less about proving you're right or wrong and more about seeing others draw closer to the unconditional love of Jesus?

I am the kind of person who wants everybody to get along. I have the kind of faith that doesn't want to exclude people. It bothers me when someone hurts another person. So the word tolerance is a word I liked until I started reading the Scriptures. Can tolerance and faith coexist? The Bible is very clear that people will have different beliefs than you and that others will not take it lightly. We know that because:

- Romans 1:18-25 says that God gives us all evidence that He is true.
- John 14:6 says that Jesus is the only way among all other spiritual paths.
- Luke 6:22 says that we are blessed when others reject us.
- John 15:18 says that when the world hates you, they hated Christ first.

These Scriptures are clear: people are not always going to agree with you and will even get hostile because faith in God is exclusive through Jesus. So how do we respond to this reality as Christ followers in a tolerance culture?

14: IT'S NOT ABOUT BEING POLITICALLY MOTIVATED BUT INSTEAD BEING GOSPEL FOCUSED.

Gospel means "good news." So be a bringer of "good news" not "bad news" or "fake news." You can't have the gospel without grace. We need the graciousness of God. So be a gracious person. Graciousness is one of the most potent postures you can make when engaging with others. Graciousness overrules combativeness at the end of the day. The Bible says this about graciousness, "Let your conversation be gracious and attractive so that you will have the right response for everyone" (Colossians 4:6).

It's hard to resist a kind person. It's hard to be hostile towards a compassionate person. It's difficult to deny someone who forgives readily. How Jesus dealt with differing opinions is how we should deal with opinions that are different from ours. Jesus was gracious, and graciousness is a stronger and better choice than tolerance. Graciousness is defined as having a forgiving attitude and compassionate posture as you walk in wisdom with those whose opinions, attitudes and beliefs are different than yours.

Jesus faced popular opposition in His day. In one case, when confronted with stubborn, unredeemed and resistant people, Jesus is said to have been angry at their stance. Mark says Jesus "looked around at them angrily and was deeply saddened by their hard hearts" (Mark 3:5). This the the only time we see Jesus angry and perform a miracle at the same time. So how does Jesus channel His anger and sadness at their ignorance? He chooses to be angry (without sinning, of course) and do God's will at the same time—showing us that it can be done.

Use your passion to pay it forward positively. Paul insists, "Do not repay anyone evil for evil ... do not take revenge ... do not be overcome by evil, but overcome evil with good" (Romans 12:17). Jesus' mission was to seek and save the lost. He had a fierce determination to not allow the opposition of others to sidetrack him from His purpose or to deflect Him from his mission. Peter tried to repay evil for evil by picking a battle and even hurting someone physically when he cut off a Roman guard's ear. Trying to pay back an eye for an eye or an ear for an ear is not the heart of Jesus. As a matter of fact, Jesus said to Peter, "Am I leading a rebellion?" and He healed the soldier's ear (Luke 22).

Jesus' response was healing, not hurtful. That should be our response as well. For example, do we boycott Target for instituting transgender bathrooms, or do we offer to clean the bathrooms to show the world that serving is more valuable than protesting?

The best thing you can do is love those who don't agree with you: not just pray for them, but love them (Luke 6:27). Loving your enemies means that you not only pray for them but bless them when they persecute you. It means showing kindness to those who disagree with you.

Jesus didn't just write off the Romans for their tyranny, he engaged them by going to the house of a centurion and healing his servant's son (Luke 7:1–10). While everyone was boycotting Rome's rules and regulations, Jesus was willing to go into a centurion's house with a miracle, not a reprimand or a demand.

Know who your real enemy is. We are not battling against a person but an ideology, or in spiritual terms, a stronghold or pattern of belief. As Christians, we must know that our opponents are not our real enemies. We must regularly remind ourselves of the real war going on behind the scenes, as described in Ephesians 6:10–20. The real war is in the spiritual world, and it must be fought with spiritual weapons.

Our real enemies are spiritual: "principalities ... powers ... the rulers of the darkness of this world." Our perceived "human enemies" are confused, misunderstood and even being held captive by the real enemy of our souls.

It's important to pursue a change of heart, not a change of opinion. Jesus took the initiative when things got heavy and when others pushed back. He stood up to His opponents with grace and truth. But He didn't fight on their terms, but on His terms. He turned the tables ... strategically and literally.

Jesus was more concerned with the heart of someone than their political opinion. He took the controversy to them. He appealed to their logic as well as their conscience. That's why, for example, he posed the question, "Which is easier: to say, 'Your sins are forgiven,' or to say, 'Get up and walk?'" (Luke 5:23).

Jesus sought not to win arguments, but to change hearts and minds. His desire was to bring them to a place of surrender so that they could experience forgiveness. And that must be our motivation; that "they may see [our] good deeds and praise [our] Father in heaven" (Matt. 5:16).

Always let the Holy Spirit lead you. What does it look like for you to love a transgender individual, an addicted teenager, a liberal, a Republican, the girl who is living with her boyfriend, your gay neighbors, your porn-addicted friend, the person who believes that all roads lead to heaven and thinks that you are narrow-minded? In the words of Paul:

> Love is patient and kind. Love is not jealous or boastful or proud or rude. It does not demand its own way. It is not irritable, and it keeps no record of being wronged. it does not rejoice about injustice but rejoices whenever the truth wins out. Love never gives up, never loses faith, is always hopeful, and endures through every circumstance (1 Corinthians 13:4–7).

First Corinthians 13 is not about marriage (sorry well-meaning people), but spiritual gifts. It's about enabling the Holy Spirit to use you to make a difference in the people around you—and to make a difference, you need love. If you don't have love as you engage others, you are nothing. Plain and simple. The love Paul describes isn't a passive love. It's quite the opposite, actually. It's an aggressive love because it speaks about the moments you'll have to love people who exhibit boasting and passionate disagreement.

That's why we get a list of words, like patience, kindness and not holding grudges. Because this is in the context of the Holy Spirit: Only He can give you this kind of love, this kind of mindset, and this kind of heart for others.

For you to be a gift and a blessing to those around you, let the Holy Spirit give you the ability to respond according to this Scripture, and watch the outrage around you lose strength. God's Spirit of Truth will always be stronger than the outrage of culture.

Always.

CHAPTER 9 QUESTIONS

1. On a scale of 1 to 10 (1 being civil and 10 being being outrageous), what would you give as our current level of outrage in culture right now?

2. While turning the other cheek seems like the right thing to do, resisting retaliation and choosing forgiveness is hard. Which of those two options is harder? Easier? Why?

3. What does "going the extra mile" as you are living under an authority (political, professional, relational, etc) you don't agree with look like?

4. Can you show honor to someone you don't like or agree with? Why? Did Jesus?

5. Can you do better at living in the "in-between"?

6. Read Daniel 1:8-9; 20. How did Daniel choose outreach over outrage? What does that look like today?

6. Are people having more confrontations or conversations today?

ACKNOWLEDGMENTS

I truly believe the world is a better place because of Christians and the Church. This has been my life since I was 22 years old when I gave my life to Jesus Christ. My journey has led me across many people who have taken a chance on me and believed in me when I didn't believe in myself. Without the experiences and the support of the churches and the leadership who have taken their time and effort to invest in me, this book wouldn't exist. My faith is what it is today because of the mentorship, encouragement and investment of so many. Thank you to Pastor Rob Ketterling and River Valley Church for letting me be on the journey with you since 2004, showing me what exceptional leadership can look like and always inspiring me to change the world. Thank you to Mark Batterson for risking it all to start National Community Church and being a "hero in the faith" to me and so many. Thank you to Pastor Aaron Fruh who spoke into me that I have it in my future to be an author and for giving me my Mobile years. Thank you to Pastor Brad and Becky Davis for being the first pastors I ever had and for loving me through the years. Thank you to all the students I had the privilege of pastoring in my years as a youth pastor and for showing me grace while allowing me to be a voice of encouragement and inspiration in your lives – it was and will always be an honor to know you and love you. Thank you to my very special "sons and daughters in the faith" for letting me be a "father in the faith" to you all-you are all so incredibly special to me and

I look forward to celebrating many more years together on our journey. Thanks to one of my best friends, Brian Engl, for inspiring me when I didn't feel inspired and for letting me be me. Thank you to Erik and Diane Skoog for showing me the church and the world is bigger than the small town I came from. Thank you to Mom and Dad Mattson for loving me like a son. Thank you to Mike Tomsche for being a friend to me from the beginning and holding on to our friendship through the years.

Thank you to my mom, my dad and my brother for loving me and for always being my family.

Having an idea and turning it into a book is as hard as it sounds. The experience is both internally challenging and rewarding. I especially want to thank the individuals that helped bring this project to life: Erik Swenson, Claire Rogers, Vince Brown, Brett Knutson, Samuel Deuth. Your hard work, time and determination, wise counsel at the right time and devotion to this project will always be unforgettable.